W9-BUH-898

ENGLISH MEN OF LETTERS

JOHN GREENLEAF WHITTIER

·The MC Co·

ENGLISH MEN OF LETTERS

John Greenleaf Whittier

BY

THOMAS WENTWORTH HIGGINSON

New York
THE MACMILLAN COMPANY
LONDON: MACMILLAN & CO., LTD.
1911

All rights reserved

811.3
W625Whi

SUBEO UT PROSIM · ACADEMIA · BRADFORDENSIS · CONDITA A.D. 1804

Copyright, 1902,

By THE MACMILLAN COMPANY.

Set up and electrotyped. Published October, 1902. Reprinted July, 1907; January, 1911.

L.C. 02-26525

Norwood Press
J. S. Cushing Co. — Berwick & Smith Co.
Norwood, Mass., U.S.A.

OCLC 1171639

12

6744

NOTE

The thanks of the author are due to various friends and correspondents who have aided him with information or criticism; and especially to his friend Samuel T. Pickard, Esq., the authorized biographer of Whittier, whose invaluable work must always hold the leading place among all books relating to the poet's personal history, and who has also been most generous in the way of private counsel.

T. W. H.

Cambridge, Mass.

CONTENTS

JOHN GREENLEAF WHITTIER

JOHN GREENLEAF WHITTIER

CHAPTER I

CHILDHOOD

The American traveller in England who takes pains to inquire in bookstores as to the comparative standing of his country's poets among English readers, is likely to hear Longfellow ranked at the head, with Whittier as a close second. In the same way, if he happens to attend English conventions and popular meetings, he will be pretty sure to hear these two authors quoted oftener than any other poets, British or American. This parallelism in their fame makes it the more interesting to remember that Whittier was born within five miles of the old Longfellow homestead, where the grandfather of his brother poet was born. Always friends, though never intimate, they represented through life two quite different modes of rearing and education. Longfellow was the most widely travelled author of the Boston circle, Whittier the least so; Longfellow spoke a variety of languages, Whittier only his own; Longfellow had whatever the American college of his time could give him, Whittier had none of it; Longfellow had the habits of a man of the world, Whittier those of a recluse; Longfellow touched reform but lightly, Whittier was essentially imbued with it; Longfellow had children and grandchildren, while Whittier led a single life. Yet in certain gifts, apart from poetic quality, they were alike; both being modest, serene, unselfish, brave, industrious, and generous. They either shared, or made up between them, the highest and most estimable qualities that mark poet or man.

Whittier, like Garrison, — who first appreciated his poems, — was brought up apart from what Dr. Holmes loved to call the Brahmin class in America; those, namely, who were bred to cultivation by cultivated parents. Emerson, Longfellow, Holmes, Lowell, were essentially of this class; all their immediate ancestors were, in French phrase, *gens de robe;* three of them being children of clergymen, and one of a lawyer who was also a member of Congress. All of them had in a degree — to borrow another phrase from Holmes — tumbled about in libraries. Whittier had, on the other hand, the early training of a spiritual aristocracy, the Society of Friends. He was bred in a class which its very oppressors had helped to ennoble; in the only meetings where silence ranked as equal with speech, and women with men; where no precedence was accorded to anything except years and saintliness; where no fear was felt but of sin. This gave him at once the companionship of the humble and a habit of deference to those whom he felt above him; he had measured men from a level and touched human nature directly in its own vigour and yet in its highest phase. Not one of this eminent circle had the keys of common life so absolutely in his hands as Whittier. Had anything been wanting in this respect, his interest in politics would have filled the gap. First thrilled by the wrongs of the slave, and serving in that cause a long apprenticeship, it was instinctive in him to be the advocate of peace, of woman suffrage, of organised labour. In such outworks of reform he had an attitude, a training, and a sympathy which his literary friends had not. He was, in the English phrase, "a poet of the people," and proved by experience that even America supplied such a function. Not in vain had he studied the essential dignity of the early New England aristocracy, as he traced the lineage of his heroine, Amy Wentworth, and paced with her the streets of Portsmouth, N.H., a region less wholly Puritan than Massachusetts: —

> "Her home is brave in Jaffrey Street,
> With stately stairways worn
> With feet of old Colonial knights
> And ladies gentle-born.
>
> * * * * * *
>
> "And on her, from the wainscot old,
> Ancestral faces frown, —
> And this has worn the soldier's sword,
> And that the judge's gown."

All this type of life he had studied in New England history, — none better, — but what real awe did it impose on him who had learned at his mother's knee to seek the wilderness with William Penn or to ride through the howling mobs with Barclay of Ury? The Quaker tradition, after all, had a Brahminism of its own which Beacon Street in Boston could not rear or Harvard College teach. To this special privilege John Greenleaf Whittier was born in Haverhill, Mass., on Dec. 17, 1807.

The founder of the name and family of Whittier in this country, Thomas Whittier, was one of that type of ancestors to which every true American looks back with pride, if he can. Of Huguenot descent, but English training, he sailed from Southampton in 1638, and settled in what was then Salisbury, but is now Amesbury, on Powow River — the poet's "swift Powow" — a tributary of the Merrimac. He was then eighteen, and was a youth weighing three hundred pounds and of corresponding muscular strength. Later, he removed to Haverhill, about ten miles away, and built a log house near what is now called "the Whittier homestead." Here he dwelt with his wife, a distant kinswoman, whose maiden name was Ruth Flint, and who had come over with him on the packet ship. They had ten children, five of whom were boys, each of these being over six feet in height. Then he naturally built for his increasing family a larger house, "the homestead," which is still standing, and in which some of his descendants yet live. He was a leading citizen of Haverhill, which was for the greater part of a century a frontier village, subject to frequent incursions from the Indians, one of these resulting in the well-known tragedy of Hannah Dustin. From these raids Thomas Whittier never suffered, though he was one of the town committee to provide fortified houses for places of refuge in case of danger. That he never even bolted his own doors at night is the tradition of the family.

This tradition suggests the ways and purposes of the Society of Friends, but it does not appear that Thomas Whittier actually belonged to that body, though he risked name and standing to secure fair treatment for those who led it. Mr. Pickard, the poet's biographer, tells us that in 1652 he joined in petitioning the legislature, then called "general court," for the pardon of Robert Pike, who had been heavily fined for speaking against the order prohibiting certain Quakers from exhorting "on the Lord's Day," even in their own houses. Not only was this petition not granted, but the petitioners were threatened with loss of rights as "freemen" unless they withdrew their names. Sixteen refused to withdraw them, of whom two, Thomas Whittier and Christopher Hussey, were ancestors of the poet, as was one of the prohibited exhorters, Joseph Peasley. These were temporarily disfranchised, but the name of Thomas Whittier often appears with honour in the town records, even to mentioning the fact that when he came to dwell in Haverhill he brought with him a hive of bees which had been willed to him by his uncle, Henry Rolfe, a fellow passenger to this country. This hive of bees, as an emblem of industry and thrift, has been used by some of his descendants as the basis of a monogram.[1]

In the house thus honourably occupied by a manly progenitor, John Greenleaf Whittier was born, his middle name coming from his paternal grandmother, Sarah Greenleaf, about whom he wrote a ballad, and about whose name — translated, as is supposed, from the French Feuillevert — he has written the poem, "A Name." He was also descended through his maternal grandmother from Christopher Hussey, who had married a daughter of the Rev. Stephen Bachiler, a man of distinguished appearance and character, whose reputation was clouded for two centuries by charges made in his own day, but which now seem to have been dis-

[1] Pickard's "Whittier," I. 5.

pelled by his descendants.[1] Father Bachiler's striking appearance, dark, thin, and straight, black eyebrows, descended to the two men most conspicuous among his posterity, John Greenleaf Whittier and Daniel Webster.

The homestead in which Whittier was reared is to this day so sheltered from the world that no neighbour's roof has ever been in sight from it; and Whittier says of it in "Snow-Bound"

> "No church-bell lent its Christian tone
> To the savage air; no social smoke
> Curled over woods of snow-hung oak."

In a prose paper by him, moreover, "The Fish I Didn't Catch," published originally in the *Little Pilgrim*, in Philadelphia, in 1843, there is a sketch of the home of his youth, as suggestive of a rustic boyhood as if it had been made in Scotland. It opens as follows: —

"Our old homestead (the house was very old for a new country, having been built about the time that the Prince of Orange drove out James the Second) nestled under a long range of hills which stretched off to the west. It was surrounded by woods in all directions save to the southeast, where a break in the leafy wall revealed a vista of low, green meadows, picturesque with wooded islands and jutting capes of upland. Through these, a small brook, noisy enough as it foamed, rippled, and laughed down its rocky falls by our garden-side, wound, silently and scarcely visible, to a still larger stream, known as the Country Brook. This brook in its turn, after doing duty at two or three saw and grist mills, the clack of which we could hear across the intervening woodlands, found its way to the great river, and the river took it up and bore it down to the great sea.

[1] See the imputations in *Winthrop's Journal*, and the final vindication in a paper by Charles E. Batchelder in *N. E. Historical and Genealogical Register*, January, 1892.

"I have not much reason for speaking well of these meadows, or rather bogs, for they were wet most of the year; but in the early days they were highly prized by the settlers, as they furnished natural mowing before the uplands could be cleared of wood and stones and laid down to grass. There is a tradition that the hay-harvesters of two adjoining towns quarrelled about a boundary question, and fought a hard battle one summer morning in that old time, not altogether bloodless, but by no means as fatal as the fight between the rival Highland clans, described by Scott in 'The Fair Maid of Perth.' I used to wonder at their folly, when I was stumbling over the rough hassocks, and sinking knee-deep in the black mire, raking the sharp sickle-edged grass which we used to feed out to the young cattle in midwinter, when the bitter cold gave them appetite for even such fodder. . . .

"Nevertheless, the meadows had their redeeming points. In spring mornings the blackbirds and bobolinks made them musical with songs; and in the evenings great bullfrogs croaked and clamoured; and on summer nights we loved to watch the white wreaths of fog rising and drifting in the moonlight like troops of ghosts, with the fireflies throwing up ever and anon signals of their coming. But the Brook was far more attractive, for it had sheltered bathing-places, clear and white-sanded, and weedy stretches, where the shy pickerel loved to linger, and deep pools where the stupid sucker stirred the black mud with his fins. I had followed it all the way from its birthplace among the pleasant New Hampshire hills, through the sunshine of broad, open meadows, and under the shadow of thick woods. . . . Macaulay has sung, —

> "'That year young lads in Umbro
> Shall plunge the struggling sheep;'

and this picture of the Roman sheep-washing recalled, when we read it, similar scenes in the Country Brook."[1]

The house still stands in which Whittier thus dwelt. It has an oaken frame, composed of timber fifteen inches

[1] Whittier's "Works," V. 320–22.

square; it is about thirty-six feet long, and is built around a central chimney. The kitchen, which is the chief room, is thirty feet long, and the fireplace is eight between the jambs. The latest houses built by wealth in the rural parts of New England are essentially modelled as to their large rooms from these old colonial houses. The enormous labour required in tempering the cold in these elder dwellings — for warmed throughout they never were — cannot easily be recognized in the modern, which rely on the open fireplaces only for spring and autumn, and on furnaces for the rest. How much more real and genuine seems the conflict with frost and snow upon Whittier's hearth. He describes, in "Snow-Bound," the building of the fire: —

"We piled, with care, our nightly stack
Of wood against the chimney-back —
The oaken log, green, huge, and thick,
And on its top the stout back-stick;
The knotty fore-stick laid apart,
And filled between with curious art
The ragged brush; then, hovering near,
We watched the first red blaze appear,
Heard the sharp crackle, caught the gleam
On whitewashed wall and sagging beam,
Until the old, rude-furnished room
Burst, flower-like, into rosy bloom;
While radiant with a mimic flame
Outside the sparkling drift became,
And through the bare-boughed lilac tree
Our own warm hearth seemed blazing free.
The crane and pendent trammels showed,
The Turk's heads on the andirons glowed;
While childish fancy, prompt to tell
The meaning of the miracle,

Whispered the old rhyme, 'Under the tree,
When fire outdoors burns merrily,
There the witches are making tea.'"

He next paints for us the group around the fireside:—

"Shut in from all the world without,
We sat the clean-wingèd hearth about,
Content to let the north-wind roar
In baffled rage at pane and door,
While the red logs before us beat
The frost-line back with tropic heat;
And ever, when a louder blast
Shook beam and rafter as it passed,
The merrier up its roaring draught
The great throat of the chimney laughed;
The house-dog on his paws outspread
Laid to the fire his drowsy head,
The cat's dark silhouette on the wall
A couchant tiger's seemed to fall;
And, for the winter fireside meet,
Between the andirons' straggling feet,
The mug of cider simmered slow,
The apples sputtered in a row,
And, close at hand, the basket stood
With nuts from brown October's wood."

Here we have, absolutely photographed, the Puritan Colonial interior, as it existed till within the very memory of old men still living. No other book, no other picture preserves it to us; all other books, all other pictures combined, leave us still ignorant of the atmosphere which this one page re-creates for us; it is more imperishable than any interior painted by Gerard Douw. And this picture we owe to a lonely invalid, who painted it in memory of his last household companions, his mother and his sister.

It must be remembered that, in the poet's childhood, the yearly meetings of the Society of Friends at Amesbury were relatively large, and the name of that kindly denomination was well fulfilled by the habit of receiving friends from a distance. They came in their own conveyances to Amesbury or its adjoining settlement, Haverhill, and remained for days in succession, the Whittier home entertaining sometimes as many as ten or fifteen. In such a household Whittier grew up, listening not without occasional criticism to his father's first-day readings from the Scriptures; visiting with his parents the Quarterly Meeting in Salem, passing a leafless tree, pointed out to him as that on which the witches were hung, and seeing on another drive the bridge where the drawtender had died in accordance with a previous ghostly warning. Or else he followed by the fireside his Aunt Mercy's mystic tales, when she narrated the appearance of her lover's spectre, riding on horseback, but moving away without sound of hoofs, and afterward proving to have died at the very day and hour of her vision. Or his father told tales of early trading expeditions to Canada, through the Indian-haunted woods.

"Our father rode again his ride
On Memphremagog's wooded side;
Sat down again to moose and samp
In trapper's hut and Indian camp;
Lived o'er the old idyllic ease
Beneath St. François' hemlock trees;
Again for him the moonlight shone
On Norman cap and bodiced zone;
Again he heard the violin play
Which led the village dance away,
And mingled in its merry whirl

The grandam and the laughing girl.
Or, nearer home, our steps he led
Where Salisbury's level marshes spread
  Mile-wide as flies the laden bee;
Where merry mowers, hale and strong,
Swept, scythe on scythe, their swaths along
  The low green prairies of the sea."

His mother, in her turn, pointed out the glimmering reflection of the firelight in the small, thick panes of window glass, and taught him the old rhyme about the witches making tea there, or told him of a point in the Country Brook, where there was a tradition of a witch meeting, consisting of six little old women in sky blue cloaks; or of a bridge where a teamster had once seen a ghost bobbing for eels, or other tales best recorded in the poet's own simple verse.

"Our mother, while she turned her wheel,
Or ran the new-knit stocking-heel,
Told how the Indian hordes came down
At midnight on Cochecho town,
And how her own great-uncle bore
His cruel scalp-mark to fourscore;
Recalling, in her fitting phrase,
So rich and picturesque and free,
(The common unrhymed poetry
Of simple life and country ways)
The story of her early days.
She made us welcome to her home;
Old hearths grew wide to give us room;
We stole with her a frightened look
At the gray wizard's conjuring book,
The fame whereof went far and wide
Through all the simple country side;
We heard the hawks at twilight play,
The boat-horn on Piscataqua,

The loon's weird laughter far away;
We fished her little trout-brook, knew
What flowers in wood and meadow grew,
What sunny hillsides autumn-brown
She climbed to shake the ripe nuts down;
Saw where in sheltered cove and bay
The ducks' black squadron anchored lay,
And heard the wild geese calling loud
Beneath the gray November cloud.
Then, haply with a look more grave
And soberer tone, some tale she gave
From painful Sewell's ancient tome,
Beloved in every Quaker home,
Of faith fire-winged by martyrdom,
Or Chalkley's Journal, old and quaint, —
Gentlest of skippers, rare sea-saint! —"

Or his uncle told of the "lore of fields and brooks."

"Himself to Nature's heart so near
That all her voices in his ear
Of beast or bird had meanings clear,
Like Apollonius of old,
Who knew the tales the sparrows told,
Or Hermes who interpreted
What the sage cranes of Nilus said;
A simple, guileless, childlike man,
Content to live where life began;
Strong only on his native grounds,
The little world of sights and sounds
Whose girdle was the parish bounds.

* * * * * *

He told how teal and loon he shot,
And how the eagle's eggs he got,
The feats on pond and river done,
The prodigies of rod and gun;
Till, warming with the tales he told,
Forgotten was the outside cold,

The bitter wind unheeded blew,
From ripened corn the pigeons flew,
The partridge drummed i' the wood, the mink
Went fishing down the river-brink;
In fields with bean or clover gay
The woodchuck, like a hermit gray,
Peered from the doorway of his cell.
The musk-rat plied the mason's trade,
And tier by tier his mud-walls laid;
And from the shagbark overhead
The grizzled squirrel dropped his shell."

Add to these the two young sisters; the village schoolmaster with his love of books and wandering; and add that strange, half-crazed guest, Harriet Livermore, who had been for a time a convert to the doctrines of Friends until she quarrelled with her lover on a minor point of doctrine and knocked him down with a stick of wood. She then became a preacher of the Second Advent, and travelled for years in Europe to proclaim its doctrines. Lastly, we must add such occasional guests as Whittier himself describes in this narrative: —

"On one occasion, on my return from the field at evening, I was told that a foreigner had asked for lodging during the night, but that, influenced by his dark, repulsive appearance, my mother had very reluctantly refused his request. I found her by no means satisfied with her decision. 'What if a son of mine was in a strange land?' she inquired, self-reproachfully. Greatly to her relief, I volunteered to go in pursuit of the wanderer, and, taking a cross path over the fields, soon overtook him. He had just been rejected at the house of our nearest neighbour; and was standing in a state of dubious perplexity in the street. His looks quite justified my mother's suspicions. He was an olive-complexioned, black-bearded Italian, with an eye like a live coal, such a face as perchance looks out on the traveller in the passes of the Abruzzi, one of those bandit visages which Salvator has painted. With some difficulty I gave him to understand my errand, when he overwhelmed me with thanks, and joyfully followed me back. He took his seat with us at the supper-table; and, when we were all gathered round the hearth that cold autumnal evening, he told us, partly by words, and partly by gestures, the story of his life and misfortunes: amused us with descriptions of the grape-gatherings and festivals of his sunny clime; edified my mother with a recipe for making bread of chestnuts; and in the morning, when after breakfast his dark sullen face lighted up, and his fierce eyes moistened with grateful emotion as in his own silvery Tuscan accent he poured out his thanks, we marvelled at the fears which had so nearly closed our doors against him; and, as he departed, we all felt that he had left with us the blessing of the poor."

But what was the boy himself who was nurtured by that fireside? Whittier tells us this also, in his other poem, "The Barefoot Boy."

"Blessings on thee, little man
Barefoot boy with cheek of tan,
With thy turned-up pantaloons,
And thy merry whistled tunes;
With thy red lip, redder still
Kissed by strawberries on the hill;
With the sunshine on thy face
Through thy torn brim's jaunty grace:
From my heart I give thee joy,
I was once a barefoot boy.

* * * * * *

O for boyhood's painless play,
Sleep that wakes in laughing day,
Health that mocks the doctor's rules,
Knowledge never learned in schools:

Of the wild bee's morning chase,
Of the wild flower's time and place,
Flight of fowl and habitude
Of the tenants of the wood;
How the tortoise bears his shell,
How the woodchuck digs his cell,
And the ground-mole sinks his well;
How the robin feeds her young,
How the oriole's nest is hung;
Where the whitest lilies blow,
Where the freshest berries grow,
Where the ground-nut trails its vine,
Where the wood-grape's clusters shine;
And the architectural plans
Of gray hornet artisans! —
For, eschewing books and tasks,
Nature answers all he asks;
Hand in hand with her he walks,
Face to face with her he talks,
Part and parcel of her joy;
Blessings on the barefoot boy!

"O for boyhood's time of June,
Crowding years in one brief moon,
When all things I heard or saw
Me, their master, waited for!
I was rich in flowers and trees,
Humming-birds and honey-bees;
For my sport the squirrel played,
Plied the snouted mole his spade;
For my taste the blackberry cone
Purpled over hedge and stone;
Laughed the brook for my delight,
Through the day and through the night
Whispering at the garden wall,
Talked with me from fall to fall;
Mine the sand-rimmed pickerel pond,
Mine the walnut slopes beyond,

Mine on bending orchard trees
Apples of Hesperides!
Still as my horizon grew
Larger grew my riches too;
All the world I saw or knew
Seemed a complex Chinese toy,
Fashioned for a barefoot boy.

"O for festal dainties spread,
Like my bowl of milk and bread,
Pewter spoon and bowl of wood,
On the door-stone gray and rude!
O'er me, like a regal tent,
Cloudy-ribbed the sunset bent,
Purple-curtained, fringed with gold,
Looped in many a wind-swung fold;
While for music came the play
Of the pied frog's orchestra;
And to light the noisy choir,
Lit the fly his lamp of fire.
I was monarch: pomp and joy
Waited on the barefoot boy."

Out of doors the boy took his share of the farm duties, indeed too great a share, he afterward found, for his health. Inheriting the tall figure of his predecessors, he did not inherit their full strength; he was always engaged, like them, in subduing the wilderness; he had to face the cold of winter weather in what would now be called insufficient clothing; it was before that period had arrived when, in Miss Catherine Sedgwick's phrase, the New England Goddess of Health held out flannel underclothing to everybody. The barn, as Whittier himself afterward testified, had no doors: the winter winds whistled through, and snow drifted on its floors for more than a century. There

Whittier milked seven cows; and tended a horse, two oxen, and some sheep. It would seem a healthy and invigorating boyhood, yet he was all his life a recognised invalid, although he lived to be eighty-five, five years older than any of his Whittier ancestors, who were all recorded as stalwart men.

These various associations and sources of knowledge took the place of books to the boy's mind; but every old-fashioned family of Friends had its own little bookcase, partly theological, yet also largely biographical, always carefully read. The Whittier library of thirty volumes furnished no exception to this. We have a list of the leading works, and it is characteristic of the period that these included not only some which were distinctly secular, but even some so reprehensible that they are now difficult to find, and quite banished from orderly households. One of his first attempts in verse was a rhymed catalogue of the books in the family library — a list which begins as follows:

"The Bible towering o'er all the rest,
Of all other books the best.

"William Penn's laborious writing
And a book 'gainst Christians fighting.

"A book concerning John's Baptism,
Elias Smith's Universalism.

"How Captain Riley and his crew
Were on Sahara's desert threw.

"How Rollins, to obtain the cash,
Wrote a dull history of trash.

"The lives of Franklin and of Penn,
Of Fox and Scott, all worthy men.

"The life of Burroughs, too, I've read,
As big a rogue as e'er was made.

"And Tufts, too, though I will be civil,
Worse than an incarnate devil."

Now the lives of Stephen Burroughs and Henry Tufts were the Gil Blas and even the Guzman d'Alfarache of the New England readers of a hundred years ago; the former having gone through many editions, while the latter — by far the wittier and wickeder of the two — was suppressed by the Tufts family, and not more than half a dozen copies are known to exist. Without it the entire life of the revolutionary period cannot be understood, and it helps us to comprehend the breadth and toleration of Whittier's nature, and especially the sense of humour which relieved it, when he gives a characterisation of Burroughs and Tufts that shows him to have read their memoirs.

For other books he borrowed what he could find, especially books of tragedy, of which he was always fond; and some were read to him by one of his teachers, Joshua Coffin, afterward a familiar figure for many years to the people of the neighbouring town of Newbury, whose town clerk and historian he was — a man of substantial figure, large head, cordial manners, and one of Garrison's twelve first abolitionists; a man whom I well remember in later years as being all that Whittier describes in him. The place where he is celebrated is in that delightful poem, "To My Old Schoolmaster" beginning

> "Old friend, kind friend! lightly down
> Drop time's snowflakes on thy crown!
> Never be thy shadow less,
> Never fail thy cheerfulness!"[1]

Coffin, then a young Dartmouth College student, used to read aloud on winter evenings, in the Whittier household, the poems of Burns, explaining the Scotch dialect; and finally lent the book to the boy of fourteen, who had heard it with delight. At a later time one of the Waverley novels came into his hands, probably by borrowing, and he and his young sister read it on the sly at bedtime, till their candle went out at a critical passage. Furthermore, he visited Boston in his teens as the guest of Mrs. Nathaniel Greene, one of his Batchelder kindred, there buying his first copy of Shakespeare, and being offered a ticket to the theatre by an accomplished actress, a kindness which he declined, because he had promised his mother to keep away from that fatal peril.

He summed up his experience of farming and farmers in this letter to the Essex Agricultural Society, dated "12th mo. 30, 1888."

"My ancestors since 1640 have been farmers in Essex County. I was early initiated into the mysteries of farming as it was practised seventy years ago, and worked faithfully on the old Haverhill homestead until, at the age of thirty years, I was compelled to leave it, greatly to my regret. Ever since, if I have envied anybody, it has been the hale, strong farmer, who could till his own acres, and if he needed help could afford to hire it, because he was able to lead the work himself. I have lived to see a great and favourable change in the farming population of Essex County. The curse of intemperance is now almost unknown among them;

[1] Whittier's "Works," IV. 73.

the rumseller has no mortgage on their lands. As a rule, they are intelligent, well informed, and healthy, interested in public affairs, self-respectful and respected, independent landholders, fully entitled, if any class is, to the name of gentleman. It may be said that they are not millionnaires, and that their annual gains are small. But, on the other hand, the farmer rests secure while other occupations and professions are in constant fear of disaster; his dealing directly and honestly with the Almighty is safer than speculation; his life is no game of chance, and his investments in the earth are better than in stock companies and syndicates. As to profits, if our farmers could care less for the comfort of themselves and their families, if they could consent to live as their ancestors once lived, and as the pioneers in new countries now live, they could, with their present facilities, no doubt, double their profits at the expense of the delicacies and refinements that make life worth living. No better proof of real gains can be found than the creation of pleasant homes for the comfort of age and the happiness of youth. When the great English critic Matthew Arnold was in this country, on returning from a visit in Essex County, he remarked that while the land looked to him rough and unproductive, the landlords' houses seemed neat and often elegant. 'But where,' he asked, 'do the tenants, the working people live?' He seemed surprised when I told him that the tenants were the landlords and the workers the owners."

CHAPTER II

SCHOOL DAYS AND EARLY VENTURES

THE whole story of Whittier's beginnings as a poet is like something from an old-fashioned German novel of Friendship — for instance, by Jean Paul — it was the casual discovery of a gifted boy by another barely grown to manhood, this leading to a life long friendship, occasionally clouded for a time by decided differences of opinion and action. William Lloyd Garrison, a young printer's apprentice, just embarked at twenty-one on a weekly newspaper in his native town of Newburyport, near Haverhill, published in the twelfth number some verses entitled "The Exile's Departure" and signed "W., Haverhill, June 1, 1826"; verses to which the young editor appended this note, "If 'W.' at Haverhill will continue to favour us with pieces as beautiful as the one inserted in our poetical department of to-day, we shall esteem it a favour." The poem itself, now interesting chiefly as a milestone, is as follows: —

"Fond scenes, which have delighted my youthful existence,
  With feelings of sorrow, I bid ye adieu —
A lasting adieu! for now, dim in the distance,
  The shores of Hibernia recede from my view.
Farewell to the cliffs, tempest-beaten and gray,
  Which guard the loved shores of my own native land;
Farewell to the village and sail-shadowed bay,
  The forest-crowned hill and the water-washed strand.

"I've fought for my country — I've braved all the dangers
That throng round the path of the warrior in strife;
I now must depart to a nation of strangers,
And pass in seclusion the remnant of life;
Far, far from the friends to my bosom most dear,
With none to support me in peril and pain,
And none but the stranger to drop the sad tear
On the grave where the heart-broken Exile is lain.

"Friends of my youth! I must leave you forever,
And hasten to dwell in a region unknown: —
Yet time cannot change, nor the broad ocean sever,
Hearts firmly united and tried as our own.
Ah, no! though I wander, all sad and forlorn,
In a far distant land, yet shall memory trace,
When far o'er the ocean's white surges I'm borne,
The scenes of past pleasures, — my own native place.

"Farewell, shores of Erin, green land of my fathers: —
Once more, and forever, a mournful adieu!
For round thy dim headlands the ocean-mist gathers,
And shrouds the fair isle I no longer can view.
I go — but wherever my footsteps I bend,
For freedom and peace to my own native isle,
And contentment and joy to each warm-hearted friend
Shall be the heart's prayer of the lonely Exile!"

HAVERHILL, 1825.

This poem was by Whittier, written in 1825 at the age of seventeen, and sent by his elder sister Mary for purposes of publication. The further history of its reception is thus told by Garrison in a lecture on Whittier, never printed by himself, but of which this extract is given by Garrison's biographers: —

"Going upstairs to my office, one day, I observed a letter lying near the door, to my address; which, on opening, I found to contain an original piece of poetry for my paper, the *Free Press.* The ink was very pale, the handwriting very small; and, having at that time a horror of newspaper 'original poetry,' — which has rather increased than diminished with the lapse of time, — my first impulse was to tear it in pieces, without reading it; the chances of rejection, after its perusal, being as ninety-nine to one; . . . but, summoning resolution to read it, I was equally surprised and gratified to find it above mediocrity, and so gave it a place in my journal. . . . As I was anxious to find out the writer, my post-rider one day divulged the secret — stating that he had dropped the letter in the manner described, and that it was written by a Quaker lad, named Whittier, who was daily at work on the shoemaker's bench, with hammer and lapstone, at East Haverhill. Jumping into a vehicle, I lost no time in driving to see the youthful rustic bard, who came into the room with shrinking diffidence, almost unable to speak, and blushing like a maiden. Giving him some words of encouragement, I addressed myself more particularly to his parents, and urged them with great earnestness to grant him every possible facility for the development of his remarkable genius. . . .

"Almost as soon as he could write, he [Whittier] gave evidence of the precocity and strength of his poetical genius, and when unable to procure paper and ink, a piece of chalk or charcoal was substituted. He indulged his propensity for rhyming with so much secrecy (as his father informed us), that it was only by removing some rubbish in the garret, where he had concealed his manuscripts, that the discovery was made. This bent of his mind was discouraged by his parents: they were in indigent circumstances, and unable to give him a suitable education, and they did not wish to inspire him with hopes which might never be fulfilled. . . . We endeavoured to speak cheeringly of the prospect of their son; we dwelt upon the impolicy of warring against Nature, of striving to quench the first kindlings of a flame which might burn like a star in our literary horizon — and we spoke too of fame — 'Sir,' replied his father, with an emotion which went home to our bosom like an electric shock, 'poetry will not give him *bread*.' What could we say? The fate of Chatterton, Otway, and the whole catalogue of those who had perished by neglect, rushed upon our memory, and — we were silent."[1]

The family tradition is simply that the number of the newspaper containing his contribution was thrown out, one day, by the carrier to the youthful Whittier, as he was working with his uncle on a stone wall by the roadside; and he read it with natural delight. Some days later a young man of fine appearance and bearing drove out to see him, accompanied by a young lady. This was Garrison, who had driven fourteen miles for that purpose. Whittier was in his working clothes, in the field, and it needed his sister Mary's persuasion to bring him to the house. Thus did he and Garrison first meet, and the latter expressed frankly to the elder Whittier his opinion of his son's talent, and the suggestion that the youth should be sent to a better school than Haverhill then afforded. The elder Whittier did not promptly accept this; it does not appear precisely whether from some lingering distrust of higher education, or simply from his own poverty. Whittier wrote to Garrison thirty years later (1859), recognising only the latter ground. "My father did not oppose me; he was proud of my pieces, but as he was in straitened circumstances he could do nothing to aid me. He was a man in advance of his times, remarkable for the soundness of his judgment and freedom from popular errors of thinking. My mother always encouraged me, and sympathised with me."

He sent also another poem, entitled "The Deity," an amplification of the eleventh and twelfth verses of

[1] "Garrison's Life," I. 67, 68.

the nineteenth chapter of First Kings. This was also written in 1825, and was published in the *Free Press* of June 22, 1826.[1] Mr. Garrison introduced it as follows: —

"The author of the following graphic sketch, which would do credit to riper years, is a youth of only sixteen years, who we think bids fair to prove another Bernard Barton, of whose persuasion he is. His poetry bears the stamp of true poetic genius, which, if carefully cultivated, will rank him among the bards of his country."

Other poems — or versified contributions — bore such a wide range of titles as "The Vale of the Merrimack," "The Death of Alexander," "The Voice of Time," "The Burial of the Princess Charlotte of Wales," "To the Memory of William Penn," "The Shipwreck," "Paulowna" "Memory," and the like; but it is impossible now to find in these the traces of genius which Garrison saw, or thought he saw; nor has their author preserved any of the above, except the first two, even in the appendix to his Riverside edition.

Later, when Garrison edited *The Journal of the Times* at Bennington, Vt., he printed in it four poems by Whittier, and wrote of him, "Our friend Whittier seems determined to elicit our best panegyrics, and not ours only, but also those of the public. His genius and situation no more correspond with each other than heaven and earth. But let him not despair. Fortune will come, ere long, 'with both hands full.'"[2] Whittier was by this time editing the *American Manufacturer* in Boston.

[1] See Whittier's "Works," IV. 334.

[2] Garrison's *Journal of the Times*, Dec. 5, 1828; "Life," I. 115.

When Garrison was in England at a great Anti-slavery Convention, that same year, Whittier wrote to him (Nov. 10, 1833): "I have, my dear Garrison, just finished reading thy speech at the Exeter Hall meeting. It is full of high and manly truth — terrible in its rebuke, but full of justice. The opening, as a specimen of beautiful composition, I have rarely seen excelled." [1]

It is to be noticed that both these young editors were the hearty supporters of what was called "Henry Clay and the American system," and that when Whittier met Clay in Washington, years after, and was asked why he did not support for office that very popular man, replied that it was because he could not support a slaveholder.[2]

The relation between Garrison and Whittier is to be further traced in this correspondence between Garrison and some young ladies in Haverhill who called themselves "Inquirers after Truth."

"W. L. GARRISON TO 'INQUIRERS AFTER TRUTH.'

"BOSTON, March 4, 1833.

"You excite my curiosity and interest still more by informing me that my dearly beloved Whittier is a *friend* and townsman of yours. Can we not induce him to devote his brilliant genius more to the advancement of our cause and kindred enterprises, and less to the creation of romance and fancy, and the disturbing incidents of political strife?"

"BOSTON, March 18, 1833.

"You think my influence will prevail with my dear Whittier more than yours. I think otherwise. If he has

[1] "Garrison's Life," I. 369, note.
[2] "Garrison's Life," I. 190.

not already blotted my name from the tablet of his memory, it is because his magnanimity is superior to neglect. We have had no correspondence whatever, for more than a year, with each other! Does this look like friendship between us? And yet I take the blame all to myself. He is not a debtor to me — I owe him many letters. My only excuse is an almost unconquerable aversion to pen, ink, and paper (as well he knows), and the numerous obligations which rest upon me, growing out of my connection with the cause of emancipation. Pray secure his forgiveness, and tell him that my love to him is as strong as was that of David to Jonathan. Soon I hope to send him a contrite epistle; and I know he will return a generous pardon."[1]

Garrison wrote after the visit to Haverhill (1833), "To see my dear Whittier once more, full of health and manly beauty, was pleasurable indeed"; and it was only three months before Whittier's pamphlet appeared entitled "Justice and Expediency; or Slavery considered with a view to its rightful remedy, Abolition."

When Garrison had urged greater school advantages for Whittier, it was a bit of advice which the elder Whittier received, as has been seen, rather coldly; but when the same counsel was given by the editor of the *Haverhill Gazette*, Mr. A. W. Thayer, and was accompanied by the offer to take the boy into his own family and let him attend the newly formed Haverhill Academy, the kind proposal was accepted. His instruction began on May 1, 1827, the necessary money having been raised by extra work done by him in making a new kind of slippers, just then invented. So carefully did Whittier plan to meet the cost of his half year's teaching, that he calculated on having

[1] "Garrison's Life," I. 331.

twenty-five cents of surplus at the end of the year, and had it.

It is an unusual thing for a newly established academy to be opened with an ode by a pupil just entered, but this was the case with the Haverhill Academy on April 30, 1827, when the oration was given by the Hon. Leverett Saltonstall of Salem. The poem cannot now be found, but we can easily test the product of the young student's muse as to quantity at least, by the columns of the *Haverhill Gazette*, which yielded forty-seven of his poems in 1827 and forty-nine in 1828. These were given under various signatures, of which "Adrian" was the chief, while "Donald," "Timothy," "Micajah," and "Ichabod" were others, and the modest initial "W." filled up the gaps. The first which appeared under his full name was a long one, "The Outlaw," printed in the *Gazette* on Oct. 28, 1828. He seems to have made an effort in early life to preserve the "Greenleaf," which was always his home name, he differing curiously at this last point from Lowell, who was always James at home and Russell, especially in England, to the world outside.

Out of all these poems written before 1829, Whittier himself preserved, in the collected edition of his works, only eight, and these in an appendix, in discouragingly small type, as if offering very little encouragement to the reader. Probably these would have passed into oblivion with the rest, had they not been, as he says in his preface, "kept alive in the newspapers for the last half-century, and some of them even in book form." They represent, the author says, "the weak beginnings of the graduate of a small country district-school, sixty years ago." "That they met with some degree of favour at that time may be accounted for by the fact that the makers of verse were then few in number, with little competition in their unprofitable vocation, and that the standard of criticism was not discouragingly high."[1]

It is curious that he here threw into this shadow of oblivion even his first long poem, "Mogg Megone," which he had nevertheless included in the first collective edition of his poems, in 1857, though saying of it in his preface that it was in a great measure composed in early life; "and it is scarcely necessary to say that its subject is not such as the writer would have chosen at any subsequent period."

An attempt was made by Mr. Thayer to get a volume containing "The Poems of Adrian" published by subscription in 1828, but this failed of success, perhaps fortunately.

The best description of Whittier's personal bearing at that time is given by one who was then a friend and associate of his younger sister, and was doubtless often at the house. This was Miss Harriet Minot, a daughter of Judge Minot of Haverhill, and afterward Mrs. Pitman of Somerville. She wrote thus of him to Mr. Francis H. Underwood, in 1883:—

"I can tell you nothing of him as a boy. I wish I could, but he is older than I, lived three miles from the village of Haverhill, where my father's home was, and was nearly nineteen years old when I first saw him. . . . He was a very handsome, distinguished-looking young man. His eyes were remarkably beautiful. He was tall, slight, and very erect, a bashful youth, but never awkward, my mother said,

[1] "Works," IV. 332.

who was a better judge than I of such matters. He went to school awhile at Haverhill Academy. There were pupils of all ages from ten to twenty-five. My brother George Minot, then about ten years old, used to say that Whittier was the best of all the big fellows, and he was in the habit of calling him 'Uncle Toby.' Whittier was always kind to children, and under a very grave and quiet exterior there was a real love of fun and a keen sense of the ludicrous. In society he was embarrassed, and his manners were in consequence sometimes brusque and cold. With intimate friends he talked a great deal and in a wonderfully interesting manner; usually earnest, often analytical, and frequently playful. He had a great deal of wit. It was a family characteristic. The study of human nature was very interesting to him, and his insight was keen. He liked to draw out his young friends, and to suggest puzzling doubts and queries.

"When a wrong was to be righted or an evil to be remedied, he was readier to act than any young man I ever knew, and was very wise in his action, shrewd, sensible, practical. The influence of his Quaker bringing-up was manifest. I think it was always his endeavour

> 'To render less
> The sum of human wretchedness.'

This, I say, was his stedfast endeavour, in spite of an inborn love of teasing. He was very modest, never conceited, never egotistic.

"One could never flatter him. I never tried; but I have seen people attempt it, and it was a signal failure. He did not flatter, but told very wholesome and unpalatable truths, yet in a way to spare one's self-love by admitting a doubt whether he was in jest or earnest.

"The great questions of Calvinism were subjects of which he often talked in those early days. He was exceedingly conscientious. He cared for people — quite as much for the plainest and most uncultivated, if they were original and had something in them, as for the most polished.

"He was much interested in politics, and thoroughly

posted. I remember, in one of his first calls at our house, being surprised at his conversation with my father upon Governor Gerry and the gerrymandering of the state, or the attempt to do it, of which I had until then been ignorant.

"He had a retentive memory and a marvellous store of information on many subjects. I once saw a little commonplace book of his, full of quaint things and as interesting as Southey's.

"His house was one of the most delightful that I ever knew, situated in a green valley, where was a laughing brook, fine old trees, hills near by, and no end of wild flowers. What did they want of the music and pictures which man makes when they had eyes to see the beauties of Nature, ears to hear its harmonies, and imaginations to reproduce them? It makes me impatient to hear people talk of the dulness and sordidness of young life in New England fifty years ago! There was Nature with its infinite variety; there were books, the best ever written, and not too many of them; there were young men and maidens with their eager enthusiasm; there were great problems to be solved, boundless fields of knowledge to explore, a heaven to believe in, and neighbours to do good to. Life was very full.

"Whittier's home was exceptionally charming on account of the character of its inmates. His father, a sensible and estimable man, died before I knew the home. His mother was serene, dignified, benevolent — a woman of good judgment, fond of reading the best books — a woman to honour and revere. His aunt, Mercy Hussey, who lived with them, was an incarnation of gracefulness and graciousness, of refinement and playfulness, an ideal lady. His sister Elizabeth, 'the youngest and the dearest,' shared his poetic gifts, and was a sweet rare person, devoted to her family and friends, kind to every one, full of love for all beautiful things, and so merry, when in good health, that her companionship was always exhilarating. I cannot imagine her doing a wrong thing or having an unworthy thought. She was deeply religious, and so were they all.

"I have said nothing of Whittier in his relations to

women. There was never a particle of coxcombry about him. He was delicate and chivalrous, but paid few of the little attentions common in society. If a girl dropped her glove or handkerchief in his presence, she had to pick it up again, especially if she did it on purpose.

"I was about to speak of his thrift and frugality, and of his independence, and of his early taking upon himself the care of the family. . . . I have not mentioned the anti-slavery cause, the subject nearest to his heart after the year 1833, the subject about which he talked most, for which he laboured most, and to which he was most devoted. All his friends became abolitionists. I was deeply in sympathy with him on this question; but this is a matter of history, and he should recount his own experience."[1]

Whittier does not preserve among his early poems "The Song of the Vermonters, 1779," published anonymously in the *New England Magazine* in 1833. He taught school in a modest way after his first half-year at the academy, then took a second and final term at the institution, partly paying his expenses by posting the ledgers of a business man in Haverhill. Through Garrison he was offered the editorship of a weekly temperance paper called *The Philanthropist*, in Boston, and wrote the following letter to his friend Thayer, asking his advice as to acceptance. It shows, better than anything else, his condition of mind at the period.

"SHAD PARISH, 28th of 11th mo., 1828.

"FRIEND A. W. THAYER, — I have been in a quandary ever since I left thee, whether I had better accept the offer of Friend Collier, or *nail* myself down to my seat, — for, verily, I could not be kept there otherwise, — and toil for the honourable and truly gratifying distinction of being considered 'a good cobbler.' . . . No — no — friend, it won't

[1] Underwood's "Whittier," 75–8.

do. Thee might as well catch a weasel asleep, or the Old Enemy of Mankind in a parsonage-house, as find me contented with that distinction.

"I have renounced college for the good reason that I have no disposition to humble myself to meanness for an education — crowding myself through college upon the charities of others, and leaving it with a debt or an obligation to weigh down my spirit like an incubus, and paralyze every exertion. The professions are already crowded full to overflowing; and I, forsooth, because I have a miserable knack of rhyming, must swell the already enormous number, struggle awhile with debt and difficulties, and then, weary of life, go down to my original insignificance, where the tinsel of classical honours will but aggravate my misfortune. Verily, friend Thayer, the picture is a dark one — but from my heart I believe it to be true. What, then, remains for me? School-keeping — out upon it! The memory of last year's experience comes up before me like a horrible dream. No, I had rather be a tin-peddler, and drive around the country with a bunch of sheepskins hanging to my wagon. I had rather hawk essences from dwelling to dwelling, or practise physic between Colly Hill and Country Bridge [the most sparsely settled portion of the East Parish].

"Seriously — the situation of editor of the *Philanthropist* is not only respectable, but it is peculiarly pleasant to one who takes so deep an interest, as I really do, in the great cause it is labouring to promote. I would enter upon my task with a heart free from misanthropy, and glowing with that feeling that wishes well to all. I would rather have the memory of a Howard, a Wilberforce, and a Clarkson than the undying fame of Byron. . . .

"I should like to see or hear from Mr. Carlton [the principal of the academy] before I do anything. He is one of the best men — to use a phrase of my craft — that ever trod shoe-leather."[1]

After leaving the academy, Whittier plunged with unexpected suddenness into journalism, which took with

[1] Pickard, I. 70.

him the form of a nursery for ardent political zeal. In Boston he was put in, as has been supposed, through Garrison's influence, as editor of the *American Manufacturer*. He was paid but nine dollars a week, half of which he saved toward paying off the mortgage on his father's farm, and he could avail himself of the Boston libraries which then seemed to him large, though they would now appear small. Then for six months he edited the *Haverhill Gazette*, and also contributed to the *New England Review* of Hartford, Conn., then edited by the once famous wit and dashing writer, George D. Prentice. The latter afterward transferred the editorship of the *New England Review* to Whittier, he himself having gone to Lexington, Ky., to write the "Life of Henry Clay," who was expecting a nomination for the Presidency. Nothing in the relation between Prentice and Whittier — the reckless man of the world and the shy young Quaker — seems quite so amusingly inappropriate as Prentice's first letter to him, ere they had even met. It runs thus: —

"Whittier, I wish you were seated by my side, for I assure you that my situation, just now, is very much to my particular satisfaction. Here am I in my hotel, with a good-natured fire in front of me, and a bottle of champagne at my left hand. Can you imagine a situation more to a good fellow's mind? . . . Then you have more imagination than judgment. . . . The gods be praised that I am not a member of the temperance society!

"Would to fortune I could come to Haverhill, before my return to Hartford — but the thing is impossible. I am running short both of time and money. Well, we can live on and love, as we have done. Once or twice I have even thought that my feelings towards you had more of romance in them than they possibly could have if we were acquainted with each other. I never yet met for the first time with a person whose name I had learned to revere, without feeling on the instant that the beautiful veil with which my imagination had robed him was partially rent away. If you cannot explain this matter, you are no philosopher."

Whittier had at Hartford more of social life than ever before, and made the acquaintance of Mrs. Sigourney, then famous; also of F. A. P. Barnard, afterward president of Columbia College.

Whittier's first thin volume, "Legend of New England" (Hartford, Hanmer and Phelps, 1831), was published with some difficulty at the age of twenty-four; and was suppressed in later life by the author himself, he buying it up, sometimes at the price of five dollars a copy, in order that he might burn it. It gave little promise, either in its prose or verse, and showed, like the early works of Hawthorne, the influence of Irving. The only things preserved from it, even in the appendix to his collected poems, are two entitled "Metacom" and "Mount Agioochook";[1] and he has wisely preserved nothing of the very rhetorical and melodramatic prose writing. Yet he showed in these the desire for home themes and the power to discover them. In "The Rattlesnake Hunter" the theme is an old man who devotes his life, among the mountains of Vermont, to the extirpation of rattlesnakes, one of which has killed his wife. "The Unquiet Sleeper" is based on the tradition of an old man in a New Hampshire village who died suddenly near his home, and whose cries were heard at night from the grave; the author claiming to have known people who had actually heard them. "The Spectre Ship" is from a tradition in Mather's "Magnalia." "The Mid-

[1] "Works," IV. 343–8.

night Attack" is a narrative of adventure with the Indians on the Kennebec River in 1722, on the part of Captain Harmon and thirty forest rangers. "The Human Sacrifice" records the escape of a young white girl from Indians, who are terrified by rumbling noises that proceed from a carbonate concealed in the rocks; this suggesting the "Great Carbuncle" of Hawthorne. All these themes, it will be noticed, are American and local, and hence desirable as selections; but the talent of the author was not precociously mature, like that of Hawthorne, nor did he continue in the same direction. Yet so far as the selection of the themes went, his work was a contribution to the rising school of native literature.

Aubrey de Vere once wrote to Tennyson that Sara Coleridge, daughter of the poet, had said to him that "However inferior the bulk of a young man's poetry may be to that of the poet when mature, it generally possesses some passages with a special freshness of their own, and an inexplicable charm to be found in them alone." It is just this quality which seems wanting in the earliest poems of Whittier. As we may observe in his youthful action a certain element of ordinary self-seeking and merely personal ambition which utterly vanishes in mature life, so there was, at that time, in his verses, an essentially commonplace quality which he himself recognised at a later time by his destruction of the volumes. Happy is he who has only this fault to deal with, and has no tinge of coarseness or mere frivolity for which to blush; and from all such elements Whittier was plainly free. Nevertheless, it must always remain one of the most curious facts in his intellectual history, that his first poetical efforts gave absolutely no promise of the future; he in this respect differing from all contemporary American poets — Bryant, Longfellow, Emerson, Holmes, Poe, and Lowell.

Whittier's desires in youth were almost equally divided between politics and poetry; and there presently appeared a third occupation in the form of that latent physical disease which haunted his whole life. This obliged him to give up the editorship of the *New England Review* and to leave Hartford on Jan. 1, 1832. He had been editing the "Literary Remains of J. G. C. Brainard," an early Connecticut poet, and wrote a preface, but did not see it in print until he had returned to Haverhill.

He wrote about himself thus frankly to Mrs. Sigourney (Feb. 2, 1832) as to his condition of mind and body at that period.

"I intended when I left Hartford to proceed immediately to the West. But a continuance of ill health has kept me at home. I have scarcely done anything this winter. There have been few days in which I have been able to write with any degree of comfort. I have indeed thrown together a poem of some length, the title of which ('Moll Pitcher') has very little connection with the subject. This poem I handed to a friend of mine, and he has threatened to publish it. It will not have the advantage or disadvantage of my name, however. I have also written, or rather begun to write, a work of fiction, which shall have for its object the reconciliation of the North and the South, — being simply an endeavour to do away with some of the prejudices which have produced enmity between the Southron and the Yankee. The style which I have adopted is about halfway between the abruptness of Laurence Sterne and the smooth gracefulness of W. Irving. I may fail, — indeed, I suspect I shall, — but I have more philosophy than poetry in my composition, and if I am disappointed in one project, I have only to lay it aside and take another up. If I thought I deserved half the compliments you have been pleased to bestow upon my humble exertions, I should certainly be in danger of becoming obnoxious to the charge of vanity. The truth is, I love poetry, with a love as warm, as fervent, as sincere, as any of the more gifted worshippers at the temple of the Muses. I consider its gift as something holy, and above the fashion of the world. In the language of Francis Bacon, 'The Muses are in league with time,' — which spares their productions in its work of universal desolation. But I *feel* and know that

> 'To other chords than mine belong
> The breathing of immortal song.'

And in consequence, I have been compelled to trust to other and less pleasant pursuits for distinction and profit. Politics is the only field now open for me, and there is something inconsistent in the character of a poet and modern politician. People of the present day seem to have ideas similar to those of that old churl of a Plato, who was for banishing all poets from his perfect republic."[1]

"Moll Pitcher" was published (Boston, 1832) anonymously, and again, but this time with his name, eight years later, together with "The Minstrel Girl" (Philadelphia, 1840). Neither of these has been included in his collected works. No American poet whose fame outlived him had ever produced in early life so much verse which he was ready to forget. On the other hand, he evidently had support all ready for him should he seriously enter public life. He wrote to his friend Jonathan Law in 1832, speaking of this: "My prospects are too good to be sacrificed for any uncertainty. I have done with poetry and literature. I can *live* as a farmer, and that is all I ask at present.

[1] Pickard, pp. 100–2.

I wish you could make me a visit, you and Mrs. Law; our situation is romantic enough — out of the din and bustle of the village, with a long range of green hills stretching away to the river; a brook goes brawling at their foot, overshadowed with trees, through which the white walls of our house are just visible. In truth, I am as comfortable as one can well be, always excepting ill health."

Mr. Pickard informs us that it is made clear by his other correspondents that the prospects of which Whittier speaks are in the line of political promotion; and that he was prevented from accepting the offer by his friends of a nomination for Congress, only because he was below what he supposed to be the legal age, twenty-five.[1]

[1] Pickard, I. 118.

CHAPTER III

WHITTIER THE POLITICIAN

As Whittier was a writer for the press before he attended a high school, so he was a politician before he was a reformer. The most surprising revelation made by Mr. Pickard's late biography of Whittier was of the manner in which he, like many promising young Americans, was early swept into political work of a really demoralising description from which only the antislavery movement withdrew him. So closely were the two phases allied, that at the very moment (1833) when he was writing and printing at his own expense an antislavery pamphlet on "Justice and Expediency," he was aiding to support a well-known public man, Caleb Cushing, for whom those two phases were apparently only dice to play with. Fortune offering for Whittier an advancement in a similar manner, he escaped the great peril by a hair's breadth. His biographer faces frankly this curious early phase in the poet's life, and volunteers the remark: "His few years in practical politics had fostered an ambition for power and patronage of which those can have no idea who only knew him after he had devoted himself to philanthropic labours." This is shown irresistibly in a letter written when there seemed a chance of his being sent as a Representative to Congress. This was the situation in brief. Congressional elections had at that time to be determined, in Massachusetts, by a majority over all other candidates, not as now by a mere plurality. In the district where he dwelt, Caleb Cushing was the candidate, and Whittier had himself supported him; but seventeen attempts at election had been successively made, without securing a majority, so that Cushing himself was probably willing that Whittier, a far more popular candidate, should be tried. The difficulty was that at the next trial, already appointed for November, Whittier would be under the required age, twenty-five. To meet this difficulty, the youth made the following proposal, it being understood that Mr. Thayer, who is mentioned, was a leading editor in the district, and had opposed Cushing, but was ready to support Whittier. Mr. Kittredge, also mentioned, was another rival candidate. The letter is dated East Parish, Wednesday morning, and was probably written in August, 1832.

"Since conversing with you yesterday, a new objection to our project has occurred to me, — the Constitution requires that the Representative shall be twenty-five years of age. I shall not be twenty-five till the 17th of December. So that I would not be eligible at the *next* trial in November. This, you will see, gives a different aspect to the whole affair. *Perhaps*, however, if the contest is *prolonged* till after the next time, the project might be put in execution.

"Suppose you advocate a holding on to Mr. C. in your Newburyport letter? Suppose, too, that you nominate in your paper Mr. Cushing without any one-sided convention? After the trial in November, you can *then* use the arguments in favour of our plan which you propose to do now; and if it suits Mr. C., he can then *request* his friends to give their votes for some other individual for the sake of promoting peace in the district. The Kittredge committee would in that case probably nominate a candidate, — if one could be found, — but, I understand Mr. Thayer, not with the expectation of his being elected.

"If I were nominated after the November trial, Mr. Thayer, situated as he and I relatively are, would support the nomination, and let the other candidate go, as he did John Merrill. Purdy, the 'Telegraph,' and the 'Essex Register' would do the same.

"The truth of the matter is, the thing would be peculiarly beneficial to me, — if not at home, it would be so abroad. It would give me an opportunity of seeing and knowing our public characters, and in case of Mr. Clay's election, might enable me to do something for myself or my friends. It would be worth more to me *now*, young as I am, than almost any office after I had reached the meridian of life.

"In this matter, if I know my own heart, I am not entirely selfish. I never yet *deserted a friend*, and I never will. If my friends enable me to acquire influence, it shall be exerted for *their benefit*. And give me once an opportunity of exercising it, my first object shall be to evince my gratitude by exertions in behalf of those who had conferred such a favour upon me.

"If you write to Newburyport to-day, you can say that we are willing and ready to do all we can at the next trial; say, too, that the Kittredge folks will scarcely find a candidate, and that there may be a chance for Cushing better than he has yet had; that at all events, it can do no harm; and that if after that trial Mr. C. sees fit to request his friends not to vote for him for the 22nd Congress, there will be as good a chance then of electing a Cushing man as there is now. Say, too, if you please, that I am ready to go on with the contest, and you had better recommend mildness in the process of electioneering.[1]"

There are many lapses from a high standard which count for less at twenty-four than at thirty; and what strikes the reader is not so much that Whittier should wish to go to Congress at that early age, as that his

[1] Pickard's "Whittier," 168, 169.

plans were based on the very methods, from which we have been trying of late years to get free — the appeal to mutual self-interest in securing posts of honour. The italics in the letter are Whittier's own; they are the points on which he wished to dwell. They would seem to imply a selfishness of nature which nothing else in his life indicates; and the only fact in his later life, with which they seem to bear the slightest connexion, is that which might otherwise have passed unobserved, namely, that he never seems to have identified himself — among the various reforms which enlisted him — with the Civil Service Reform.

Nothing, however, came of this. Cushing succeeded in being elected in 1834, and Whittier showed political skill on its best side in making Cushing the medium through which antislavery measures could be presented to Congress, when no other conspicuous member except John Quincy Adams would venture on this. Cushing was practically elected through Whittier three times in succession; but the latter gradually lost all faith in him, and when Cushing at last tried to suppress his own antislavery record, that he might get an office when the Whigs came into power in 1841, Whittier was too strong for him, reprinted the letter which under his own management had carried Cushing through his last election to Congress, and prefaced it with such skill as absolutely to defeat Cushing's ambition.

The result was that the National Senate, still largely under the influence of the slave power, three times rejected Cushing's nomination as Secretary of the Treasury, as it had previously rejected Edward Everett on the same ground, because he too had coquetted with the rising Antislavery party. The skill of Whittier — just the kind of strategetical skill which is rare among reformers — thus made itself formidable. The same thing was felt ten years later in the management which put Charles Sumner in the United States Senate; and by a curious coincidence, Caleb Cushing, who was then a member of the Legislature, was again arrayed against Whittier, and again failed.

The important local ordeal of 1848 which resulted in the downfall of the old Whig party in Massachusetts, and the substitution of what was then called the "Coalition" of the Free Soil and Democratic parties, placing Charles Sumner in the United States Senate, practically for life — this interested Whittier profoundly. I remember well that though he never made a speech in that contest, I always heard his political instinct and foresight fully recognised by my elder brothers, who regarded the other leaders — C. F. Adams, R. H. Dana, J. G. Palfrey — as too academic or unpractical for success. I, taking some personal part in the contest, as a novice, and speaking at "Free Soil" meetings which Whittier attended, remember that he watched me very closely, criticising and, when he could, commending; indeed, usually overrating the little efforts of young speakers, as non-speakers are apt to do. Thus he wrote me after my very first effort, when I emerged with difficulty from the formidable ordeal of following the mighty Sumner: "Thy address here was liked well, notwithstanding thy misgivings. Courage. Go on and prosper. Yours truly, J. G. W." And again later, in indorsement of an invitation to speak at East Salisbury (Oct. 27, 1848): "We hope thou wilt aid us in this movement [it is to be noticed that he does not use the Quaker form, 'thee will'] as we wish to make a good demonstration. I hear a fine report of thy labour in W. Amesbury and Haverhill. *Good was done.* J. G. Whittier." Such kindly words from a man of forty to a callow youth of four and twenty suggest a gratitude for which time brings no forgetfulness; at least, when that man is Whittier.

On April 24, 1850, Charles Sumner was elected United States Senator from Massachusetts, on the twenty-sixth ballot, by a majority of one. Whittier, who had taken his accustomed quiet but eager share in all the preliminary negotiations, wrote thus to his friend, Mrs. Lippincott, — known as "Grace Greenwood" in literature, — giving his view of the matter.

"I am slowly recovering from the severest illness I have known for years, the issue of which, at one time, was to me exceedingly doubtful. Indeed, I scarcely know now how to report myself, but I am better, and full of gratitude to God that I am permitted once more to go abroad and enjoy this beautiful springtime. The weather now is delightfully warm and bright, and the soft green of the meadows is climbing our hills. It is luxury to live. One feels at such times terribly rooted to this world: old Mother Earth seems sufficient for us. . . . After a long trial and much anxiety, our grand object in Massachusetts has been attained. We have sent Charles Sumner into the United States Senate, — a man physically and spiritually head and shoulders above the old hackneyed politicians of that body. The plan for this was worked out last summer at Phillips Beach, and I sounded Sumner upon it the evening we left you at that place. He really did not want the office, but we forced it upon him. I am proud of old Massachusetts, and thankful that I have had an humble share in securing her so true and worthy a representative of her honour, her freedom, and intellect, as Charles Sumner. He is a noble and gifted man, earnest and truthful. I hope great things of him, and I do not fear for his integrity and fidelity, under any trial. That Sims case was particularly mean on the part of the Boston shopkeepers. I never felt so indignant as when I saw the courthouse in chains."[1]

This last reference was to the rendition of Thomas Sims, a fugitive slave, during the progress of whose case, at the Boston Court-house, the doors were protected by chains.

In July, 1854, Whittier was invited by Ralph Waldo Emerson and others, to attend a meeting of the friends of freedom in Boston, to form a new party organization, from men from both political folds; this being one of the meetings which led to the formation of the Republican party. His reply, addressed to Emerson ("Amesbury, 3rd 7th month"), was as follows: —

"The circular signed by thyself and others, inviting me to meet you at Boston on the 7th inst., has just reached me. If I am able to visit Boston on that day, I shall be glad to comply with the invitation. Your movement I regard as every way timely and expedient. I am quite sure good will come of it, in some way. I have been for some time past engaged in efforts tending to the same object, — the consolidation of the antislavery sentiment of the North. For myself, I am more than willing to take the humblest place in a new organization made up from Whigs, anti-Nebraska Democrats, and Free-soilers. I care nothing for names; I have no prejudices against Whig or Democrat; show me a party cutting itself loose from slavery, repudiating its treacherous professed allies of the South, and making the *protection of Man* the paramount object, and I am ready to go with it, heart and soul. The great body of the people

[1] Pickard's "Whittier," I. 355, 356.

of all parties here are ready to unite in the formation of a new party. The Whigs especially only wait for the movement of the men to whom they have been accustomed to look for direction. I may be mistaken, but I fully believe that Robert C. Winthrop holds in his hands the destiny of the North. By throwing himself on the side of this movement he could carry with him the Whig strength of New England. The Democrats here, with the exception of two or three office-holders and their dependents, defend the course of Banks, and applaud the manly speeches of Sumner."[1]

I have gone a little in advance of the development of this part of Whittier's nature — that of the politician — to show how the gift which at first seemed to threaten him with moral danger became, in its gradual development, a real service to the cause of freedom. We must now return, however, to the birth of the anti-slavery movement itself, and the way in which it took control of Whittier, and pressed all his gifts, ideal and practical, into its service.

[1] Pickard's "Whittier," I. 374.

CHAPTER IV

ENLISTMENT FOR LIFE

By an interesting coincidence the first man who had encouraged Whittier in literature became his leader in reforms. William Lloyd Garrison, who had sought him at the plough as a boy, sought him a little later for a more important aim, when he encouraged him to leave all and become an ally of the antislavery movement. Whittier had already published more than a hundred poems with fair success; he had made friends in politics and was regarded as a young man of promise in that direction. But he published in the *Haverhill Gazette* in November, 1831, a poem, "To William Lloyd Garrison," and from that time forward his career was determined.

In 1830, about the time when Whittier took the editorship of the *New England Review*, Garrison had been imprisoned in Baltimore as an abolitionist; in January, 1831, the *Liberator* had been established; in 1833 Whittier had printed an anti-slavery pamphlet. In doing this he had bid farewell to success in politics and had cast in his lot, not merely with slaves, but with those who were their defenders even to death. Of these none came nearer to him, or brought home to him, at the very beginning, the possible outcome of his own career, than Dr. Reuben Crandall of Washington, who was arrested for the crime of merely lending Whittier's pamphlet to a brother physician, for which offence he was arrested in 1834, and was "confined in the old city prison until his health was destroyed, and he was liberated only to die." The fact is mentioned in "Astræa at the Capital," where Whittier says: —

"Beside me gloomed the prison cell
Where wasted one in slow decline,
For uttering simple words of mine,
And loving freedom all too well."

Whittier had been at first friendly, like Garrison, to the Colonisation Society, and had believed heartily in the future services to freedom of the then popular and always attractive statesman, Henry Clay. In June, 1834, however, he had become convinced that both Clay and the colonisation movement were in the wrong, although up to 1837, it seems, he wrote a private letter to Clay, urging him to come out against that whole enterprise.

He received from Garrison, in 1833, an invitation to attend as a delegate the National Anti-slavery Convention, to be held in Philadelphia in December. In answer to this call, he wrote to Garrison from Haverhill, Nov. 11, 1833: —

"Thy letter of the 5th has been received. I long to go to Philadelphia, to urge upon the members of my Religious Society the duty of putting their shoulders to the work — to make their solemn testimony against slavery visible over the whole land — to urge them by the holy memories of Woolman, and Benezet, and Tyson, to come up as of old to the standard of Divine Truth, though even the fires of another persecution should blaze around them. But the expenses of the journey will, I fear, be too much for me: as thee know, our farming business does not put much cash in our pockets.

I am, however, greatly obliged to the Boston Y[oung] M[en's] Association for selecting me as one of their delegates. I do not know how it may be, — but whether I go or not, my best wishes and my warmest sympathies are with the friends of Emancipation. Some of my political friends are opposed to my antislavery sentiments, and perhaps it was in some degree owing to this that, at the late Convention for the nomination of Senators for Essex, my nomination was lost by one vote. I should have rejoiced to have had an opportunity to coöperate personally with the abolitionists of Boston. . . . Can thee not find time for a visit to Haverhill before thee go on to Philadelphia? I wish I was certain of going with thee. At all events, *do* write immediately on receiving this, and tell me when thee shall start for the Quaker City."[1]

The obstacle being removed by the generosity of Samuel E. Sewall, afterward a lifelong colaborer with Whittier in the antislavery movement, the latter went to the convention, to which he was the youngest delegate. The party travelled in stage-coaches, and Whittier doubtless felt, as did the young Keats on his first visit to the North of England, as if he were going to a tournament. Of the sixty members in the convention, twelve were from Massachusetts, and twenty-one were members of the Society of Friends. Whittier was one of the secretaries and also one of the sub-committee of three which passed their Declaration of Independence. All this shows clearly the prestige which the young man had already attained, although this again was due largely to the leader of the convention, Garrison. In a paper published in the *Atlantic Monthly*, forty years later (February, 1874), Whittier gave his own reminiscence of this important experience, and from this I make a few extracts, recalling vividly the event: —

[1] "Garrison's Life," I. 393–94.

"In the gray twilight of a chill day of late November, forty years ago, a dear friend of mine residing in Boston made his appearance at the old farmhouse in East Haverhill. He had been deputed by the abolitionists of the city, William L. Garrison, Samuel E. Sewall, and others, to inform me of my appointment as a delegate to the Convention to be held in Philadelphia for the formation of an American Antislavery Society, and to urge upon me the necessity of my attendance.

"Few words of persuasion, however, were needed. I was unused to travelling; my life had been spent on a secluded farm, and the journey, mostly by stage-coach, was really a formidable one. Moreover, the few abolitionists were everywhere spoken against, their persons threatened, and in some instances a price set upon their heads by Southern legislatures. Pennsylvania was on the borders of slavery, and it needed small effort of imagination to picture to oneself the breaking up of the convention and maltreatment of its members. This latter consideration I do not think weighed much with me, although I was better prepared for serious danger than for anything like personal indignity. I had read Governor Trumbull's description of the tarring and feathering of his hero, MacFingal, when, after the application of the melted tar, the feather-bed was ripped open and shaken over him, until

> 'Not Maia's son with wings for ears
> Such plumes about his visage wears,
> Nor Milton's six-wing'd angel gathers
> Such superfluity of feathers,'

and I confess I was quite unwilling to undergo a martyrdom which my best friends could scarcely refrain from laughing at. But a summons like that of Garrison's bugle-blast could scarcely be unheeded by me who from birth and education held fast the traditions of that earlier abolitionism which, under the lead of Benezet and Woolman, had effaced from the Society of Friends every vestige of slaveholding. I had thrown myself, with a young man's fervid enthusiasm, into a movement which commended itself to my reason and con-

science, to my love of country and my sense of du[illegible]
and my fellow-men. . . . I could not hesitate, bu[illegible]
at once for the journey. It was necessary that [illegible]
start on the morrow, and the intervening time, wi[illegible]
allowance for sleep, was spent in providing for t[illegible]
the farm and homestead during my absence."

He wrote further of those composing the [illegible]
tion:—

"Looking over the assembly, I noticed that it w[illegible]
composed of comparatively young men; some in [illegible]
and a few beyond that period. They were nearly [illegible]
dressed, with a view to comfort rather than elegan[illegible]
of the faces turned toward me wore a look of e[illegible]
and suppressed enthusiasm; all had the earnestn[illegible]
might be expected of men engaged in an enterp[illegible]
with difficulty, and perhaps peril. The fine i[illegible]
head of Garrison, prematurely bald, was conspic[illegible]
sunny-faced young man at his side, in whom all [illegible]
tudes seemed to find expression, was Samuel J. M[illegible]
ling in his veins the best blood of the Sewalls and [illegible]
a man so exceptionally pure and large-hearted, [illegible]
tender, and loving, that he could be faithful to [illegible]
duty without making an enemy.

'The deil wad look into his face
And swear he could na wrang him.'

That tall, gaunt, swarthy man, erect, eagle-fa[illegible]
whose somewhat martial figure the Quaker coat [illegible]
little out of place, was Lindley Coates, known in [illegible]
Pennsylvania as a stern enemy of slavery; that sli[illegible]
man, intensely alive in every feature and ges[illegible]
Thomas Shipley, who for thirty years had been the [illegible]
of the free coloured people of Philadelphia, and w[illegible]
was whispered reverently in the slave-cabins of M[illegible]
the friend of the black man—one of a class pecu[illegible]
Quakerism, who, in doing what they felt to be a[illegible]
walking as the Light within guided them, knew n[illegible]

"In the gray twilight of a chill day of late November, forty years ago, a dear friend of mine residing in Boston made his appearance at the old farmhouse in East Haverhill. He had been deputed by the abolitionists of the city, William L. Garrison, Samuel E. Sewall, and others, to inform me of my appointment as a delegate to the Convention to be held in Philadelphia for the formation of an American Antislavery Society, and to urge upon me the necessity of my attendance.

"Few words of persuasion, however, were needed. I was unused to travelling; my life had been spent on a secluded farm, and the journey, mostly by stage-coach, was really a formidable one. Moreover, the few abolitionists were everywhere spoken against, their persons threatened, and in some instances a price set upon their heads by Southern legislatures. Pennsylvania was on the borders of slavery, and it needed small effort of imagination to picture to oneself the breaking up of the convention and maltreatment of its members. This latter consideration I do not think weighed much with me, although I was better prepared for serious danger than for anything like personal indignity. I had read Governor Trumbull's description of the tarring and feathering of his hero, MacFingal, when, after the application of the melted tar, the feather-bed was ripped open and shaken over him, until

> 'Not Maia's son with wings for ears
> Such plumes about his visage wears,
> Nor Milton's six-wing'd angel gathers
> Such superfluity of feathers,'

and I confess I was quite unwilling to undergo a martyrdom which my best friends could scarcely refrain from laughing at. But a summons like that of Garrison's bugle-blast could scarcely be unheeded by me who from birth and education held fast the traditions of that earlier abolitionism which, under the lead of Benezet and Woolman, had effaced from the Society of Friends every vestige of slaveholding. I had thrown myself, with a young man's fervid enthusiasm, into a movement which commended itself to my reason and conscience, to my love of country and my sense of duty to God and my fellow-men. . . . I could not hesitate, but prepared at once for the journey. It was necessary that I should start on the morrow, and the intervening time, with a small allowance for sleep, was spent in providing for the care of the farm and homestead during my absence."

He wrote further of those composing the convention: —

"Looking over the assembly, I noticed that it was mainly composed of comparatively young men; some in middle age, and a few beyond that period. They were nearly all plainly dressed, with a view to comfort rather than elegance. Many of the faces turned toward me wore a look of expectancy and suppressed enthusiasm; all had the earnestness which might be expected of men engaged in an enterprise beset with difficulty, and perhaps peril. The fine intellectual head of Garrison, prematurely bald, was conspicuous; the sunny-faced young man at his side, in whom all the beatitudes seemed to find expression, was Samuel J. May, mingling in his veins the best blood of the Sewalls and Quincys; a man so exceptionally pure and large-hearted, so genial, tender, and loving, that he could be faithful to truth and duty without making an enemy.

'The deil wad look into his face
And swear he could na wrang him.'

That tall, gaunt, swarthy man, erect, eagle-faced, upon whose somewhat martial figure the Quaker coat seemed a little out of place, was Lindley Coates, known in all eastern Pennsylvania as a stern enemy of slavery; that slight, eager man, intensely alive in every feature and gesture, was Thomas Shipley, who for thirty years had been the protector of the free coloured people of Philadelphia, and whose name was whispered reverently in the slave-cabins of Maryland as the friend of the black man — one of a class peculiar to old Quakerism, who, in doing what they felt to be a duty and walking as the Light within guided them, knew no fear, and shrank from no sacrifice. Braver man the world has not known. Beside him, differing in creed, but united with him in works of love and charity, sat Thomas Whitson, of the Hicksite school of Friends, fresh from his farm in Lancaster County, dressed in plainest homespun, his tall form surmounted by a shock of unkempt hair, the odd obliquity of his vision contrasting strongly with the clearness and directness of his spiritual insight. Elizur Wright, the young professor of a Western college, who had lost his place by his bold advocacy of freedom, with a look of sharp concentration, in keeping with an intellect keen as a Damascus blade, closely watched the proceedings through his spectacles, opening his mouth only to speak directly to the purpose. . . . In front of me, awakening pleasant associations of the old homestead in the Merrimac Valley, sat my first school-teacher, Joshua Coffin, the learned and worthy antiquarian and historian of Newbury. A few spectators, mostly of the Hicksite division of Friends, were present in broadbrims and plain bonnets."[1]

He thus describes the closing words of this historic convention, at which the whole organized antislavery movement came into being: —

"On the morning of the last day of our session, the Declaration, with its few verbal amendments, carefully engrossed on parchment, was brought before the convention. Samuel J. May rose to read it for the last time. His sweet, persuasive voice faltered with the intensity of his emotions as he repeated the solemn pledges of the concluding paragraphs. After a season of silence, David Thurston, of Maine, rose as his name was called by one of the secretaries, and affixed his name to the document. One after another passed up to the platform, signed, and retired in silence. All felt the deep responsibility of the occasion; the shadow and forecast of a lifelong struggle rested upon every countenance."[2]

[1] "Works," VII. 176–78.
[2] "Works," VII. 184–85.

As Whittier has himself portrayed some of the leaders in this memorable historic gathering, there should be added this delineation of his own appearance and bearing, from the graphic pen of Lowell's friend, J. Miller McKim, to whom the younger poet inscribed his own vivid picture of the later antislavery reformers: —

"He wore a dark frock coat, with standing collar, which, with his thin hair, dark and sometimes flashing eyes, and black whiskers, not large, but noticeable in those unhirsute days, gave him, to my then unpractised eye, quite as much of a military as a Quaker aspect. His broad, square forehead and well-cut features, aided by his incipient reputation as a poet, made him quite a noticeable feature of the convention."

Whittier was now enlisted for life in the antislavery body, and his feeling for Garrison reached its high-water mark at this convention; and is recorded in verses of which these are a part: —

"To W. L. G.

"Champion of those who groan beneath
  Oppression's iron hand:
In view of penury, hate, and death,
  I see thee fearless stand,
Still bearing up thy lofty brow
  In the steadfast strength of truth,
In manhood sealing well the vow
  And promise of thy youth.

"Go on — for thou hast chosen well;
  On in the strength of God!
Long as one human heart shall swell
  Beneath the tyrant's rod,

Speak in a slumbering nation's ear
  As thou hast ever spoken,
Until the dead in sin shall hear, —
  The fetter's link be broken!

"I love thee with a brother's love,
  I feel my pulses thrill,
To mark thy spirit soar above
  The cloud of human ill.
My heart hath leaped to answer thine,
  And echo back thy words,
As leaps the warrior's at the shine,
  And flash of kindred swords!" [1]

This was his first feeling toward his early friend and his last; but there were to follow long years when the internal contests of the antislavery body were scarcely less vehement and far more personally bitter than those waged with the supporters of slavery; and these cannot be passed by unnoticed. In the meantime, Whittier was enlisted for the war.

[1] "Works," III. 9.

CHAPTER V

THE SCHOOL OF MOBS

ALL this was, however, but the peaceful early stage of the antislavery moment; the mob period was approaching. It was a time peculiarly trying to those who had been bred in the non-resistance theory, and had to choose for themselves among the three alternatives, resistance, endurance, and flight. Those who in later years read the fine dramatic delineations in the poem "Barclay of Ury" do not quite appreciate the school in which Whittier learned what life meant to Barclay. The first time that actual violence came near Whittier, in his own town of Haverhill, though it missed him, was after there had been established (on April 3, 1834) an antislavery society of which he was secretary. A year or so later, in August, 1835, the Rev. Samuel J. May of Syracuse, N.Y., preached in the Unitarian pulpit at Haverhill and announced that he should give an antislavery address in the evening. The result is thus described by the historian of Haverhill: —

"The evening meeting was entirely broken up by a mob outside, who threw sand and gravel and small stones against the windows, breaking the glass, and by their hootings frightened the female portion of the audience, and led to the fear on the part of all, that more serious assaults would follow if the meeting was continued. It was therefore summarily dissolved. It was perhaps fortunate that this course was adopted, as a loaded cannon was then being drawn to the spot, to add its thunderings to the already disgraceful tumults of that otherwise quiet Sabbath evening."[1]

The preacher thus mobbed was, by universal admission, the most moderate, disarming, and courteous of all antislavery lecturers, indeed so eminent for these particular virtues as almost to constitute a class by himself. His reception shows how absolutely unjust was the charge that the abolitionists brought upon themselves, by their mere manner, the persecution they often received. In this case the meeting was broken up in uproar, and Mr. May was roughly handled as he went out, but as he had Elizabeth Whittier on one arm and her friend Harriet Minot on the other, he escaped actual violence. Less fortunate was George Thompson, the distinguished English antislavery orator, who had been the leader of the agitation for the abolition of slavery in the English colonies, and who came to America by invitation of Garrison. He acted on the fine principle laid down for all time by the so-called infidel Thomas Paine, who, when some one quoted to him the Latin motto, "Where liberty is, there is my country" (*Ubi libertas, ibi patria*) replied that this was a coward's phrase, since the brave man's watchword would be, "Where liberty is *not*, there is my country." Thompson was of course received with peculiar hostility as a foreigner, a feeling not yet extinct, for it is not many years since I saw him disdainfully classed as "a foreign carpet-bagger," and that by one of the most eminent of Boston philan-

[1] Chase's "History of Haverhill," p. 505.

thropists. He had been mobbed, accordingly, in one place after another, including Salem, whence he had escaped with difficulty and had been afterward secreted by Whittier for two weeks in East Haverhill. He and Whittier had personally undertaken a few antislavery meetings, and had set out for that purpose. I take what followed from the excellent description of their friend, Mrs. Cartland: —

" . . . Thinking themselves secure because personally unknown, the two friends drove to Plymouth, N.H., to visit Nathaniel P. Rogers, a prominent abolitionist. On their way they stopped for the night in Concord at the house of George Kent, who was a brother-in-law of Rogers. After they had gone on their way, Kent attempted to make preparations for an antislavery meeting to be held when they should return. There was furious excitement, and neither church, chapel, nor hall could be hired for the purpose. On their arrival Whittier walked out with a friend in the twilight, leaving Thompson in the house, and soon found himself and friend surrounded by a mob of several hundred persons, who assailed them with stones and bruised them somewhat severely. They took refuge in the house of Colonel Kent, who, though not an abolitionist, protected them and baffled the mob. From thence Whittier made his way with some difficulty to George Kent's, where Thompson was. The mob soon surrounded the house and demanded that Thompson and "the Quaker" should be given up. Through a clever stratagem the mob was decoyed away for a while, but, soon discovering the trick, it returned, reënforced with muskets and a cannon, and threatened to blow up the house if the abolitionists were not surrendered.

"A small company of antislavery men and women had met that evening at George Kent's, among whom were two nieces of Daniel Webster, daughters of his brother Ezekiel. All agreed that the lives of Whittier and Thompson were in danger, and advised that an effort should be made to escape. The mob filled the street, a short distance below the gate leading to Kent's house. A horse was quietly harnessed in the stable, and was led out with the vehicle under the shadow of the house, where Whittier and Thompson stood ready. It was bright moonlight, and they could see the gun-barrels gleaming in the street below them. The gate was suddenly opened, the horse was started at a furious gallop, and the two friends drove off amidst the yells and shots of the infuriated crowd. They left the city by the way of Hookset Bridge, the other avenues being guarded, and hurried in the direction of Haverhill. In the morning they stopped to refresh themselves and their tired horse. While at breakfast they found that 'ill news travels fast,' and gets worse as it goes; for the landlord told them that there had been an abolition meeting at Haverhill the night before, and that George Thompson, the Englishman, and a young Quaker named Whittier, who had brought him, were both so roughly handled that they would never wish to talk abolition again. When the guests were about to leave, Whittier, just as he was stepping into the carriage, said to the landlord, 'My name is Whittier, and this is George Thompson.' The man opened his eyes and mouth with wonder as they drove away.

"When they arrived at Haverhill they learned of the doings of the mob there, and the fortunate escape of their friend May." [1]

Another of these Thompson mobs, at which Whittier was not present, is thus described by Mrs. Lydia Maria Child, who was there. I insert her account, because it describes the period better than any other narrative I know, and gives the essential atmosphere of the life amid which Whittier was reared.

"My most vivid recollection of George Thompson is of his speaking at Julian Hall on a memorable occasion. Mr. Stetson, then keeper of the Tremont House, was present, with a large number of his slaveholding guests, who had

[1] Underwood's "Whittier," pp. 116–18.

come to Boston to make their annual purchases of the merchants. Their presence seemed to inspire Mr. Thompson. Never, even from his eloquent lips, did I hear such scathing denunciations of slavery. The exasperated Southerners could not contain their wrath. Their lips were tightly compressed, their hands clinched; and now and then a muttered curse was audible. Finally, one of them shouted, 'If we had you down South, we'd cut off your ears.' Mr. Thompson folded his arms in his characteristic manner, looked calmly at the speaker, and replied, 'Well, sir, if you did cut off my ears, I should still cry aloud, 'He that *hath* ears to hear, let him hear.'

"Meanwhile my heart was thumping like a sledge-hammer; for, before the speaking began, Samuel J. May had come to me, and said in a very low tone: 'Do you see how the walls are lined by stout truckmen, brandishing their whips? They are part of a large mob around the entrance in Federal Street, employed by the Southerners to seize George Thompson and carry him to a South Carolina vessel in waiting at Long Wharf. A carriage with swift horses is at the door, and these Southerners are now exulting in the anticipation of lynching him. But behind that large green curtain at the back of the platform there is a door leading to the chamber of a warehouse. We have the key to that door, which leads to a rear entrance of the building on Milk Street. There the abolitionists have stationed a carriage with swift horses and a coloured driver, who of course will do his best for George Thompson. Now, as soon as Mr. Thompson ceases speaking, we want antislavery women to gather round him and appear to detain him in eager conversation. He will listen and reply, but keep imperceptibly moving backward toward the green curtain. You will all follow him, and when he vanishes behind the curtain you will continue to stand close together, and appear to be still talking with him.'

"At the close of the meeting twenty-five or thirty of us women clustered around Mr. Thompson and obeyed the instructions we had received. When he had disappeared from our midst there was quiet for two or three minutes, interrupted only by our busy talking. But the Southerners soon began to stand on tiptoe and survey the platform anxiously. Soon a loud oath was heard, accompanied by the exclamation, 'He's gone!' Then such a thundering stampede as there was down the front stairs I have never heard. We remained in the hall, and presently Samuel J. May came to us, so agitated that he was pale to the very lips. 'Thank God, he is saved!' he exclaimed; and we wrung his hands with hearts too full for speech.

"The Boston newspaper press, as usual, presented a united front in sympathy with the slaveholders. . . . But they were all in the dark concerning the manner of his escape; for as the door behind the curtain was known to very few, it remained a mystery to all except the abolitionists."[1]

Garrison wrote of the Concord mob to his brother-in-law, Sept. 12, 1835, "Our brother Thompson had a narrow escape from the mob at Concord, and Whittier was pelted with mud and stones, but he escaped bodily damage." Thompson wrote to Garrison, Sept. 15: —

"You would have been delighted to have shared our adventures in *Concord* (?) on the memorable night of the 4th inst. The mirthful and the melancholy were so strangely and equally blended throughout, that I scarcely know which had the advantage, and certainly could not tell the story of our 'hairbreadth 'scapes' without exciting your risibility. However, my escape from the ignorant and murderous rabble that clamoured and thirsted for my blood was very providential, and I desire to feel grateful to Him who I believe watches over our persons and our cause, and will restrain the malice of our foes, or cause our sufferings to advance His glory.

"Poor Whittier was compelled to receive a tithe of the vengeance accumulated for me. I had really little expectation and less desire to be stoned by proxy, but such is the fruit of keeping bad company."[2]

1 Underwood's "Whittier," pp. 118–20.

2 "Garrison's Life," I. 520.

Next followed the Garrison mob, properly so called, during which Whittier happened to be in Boston, in attendance at an extra session of the state legislature, of which he was then a member. His sister being at the women's antislavery convention, he went in search of her, and found that the meeting had been broken up by a mob, or dispersed by the mayor to quiet those outside, and that the rioters had been allowed by the mayor to take down the very sign, "Female Antislavery Society" and break it to pieces, thus lynching George Thompson by proxy, as he expresses it, in a bit of harmless board. Whittier saw Garrison hurried through the street with a rope round him, and taken for safety to jail, where Whittier and May visited him in his cell; then, being warned that the house which was their own stopping-place might also be attacked, they removed Elizabeth Whittier without her knowing the reason, while they themselves mounted guard all night. This was the ordeal by which Whittier's Quaker training was tested, but it rang true. He would not arm himself, but he did not flinch where others were arming.

His courage was to be once more tested, however, in Philadelphia, while he edited the *Pennsylvania Freeman.* A hall had been erected by the antislavery people and other reformers, and was first opened on May 15, 1838. There was an address by the eminent lawyer, David Paul Brown, and a poem of a hundred and fifty lines by Whittier, whose publishing office was in the building. It was not one of his best poems, and he excluded it from his complete edition; but it was enough, with other things, to call out the gradually increasing wrath of a mob which hooted, yelled, and broke windows. On the third day the president of the Pennsylvania Hall Association called for the intervention of the mayor and sheriff. About sunset the mayor replied that, if the building were vacated and given into his possession, he would disperse the rioters. The keys were given up to him, and he addressed the mob as "Fellow-citizens." Deprecating disorder in general terms, he added: "There will be no meeting here this evening. The house has been given up to me. The managers had the right to hold the meeting, but as good citizens they have, at my request, suspended their meeting for this evening. We never call out the military here. We do not need such measures. Indeed, I would, fellow-citizens, look upon you as my police! I trust you will abide by the laws and keep order. I now bid you farewell for the night."

Since mob law began on this planet there probably was never a more dastardly invitation to outrage. Three cheers were given for the mayor, and the mob went at once to its work. Ransacking the antislavery bookstore and office, they carried all combustibles to the platform and set the building on fire. Two Southern witnesses will best tell the tale.

A Southern account of the fire appeared in a New Orleans paper, as follows: —

"At 8.30 P.M. the people, feeling themselves able and willing to do their duty, burst open the doors of the house, entered the Abolition book-store, and made complete havoc of all within. They then beat out all the windows, and, gathering a pile of window-blinds and a pile of abolition books together, they placed them under the pulpit, and set fire to them and the building. . . . The multitude, as soon as they saw the building on fire, gave a loud shout of joy.

A large number of splendid fire-engines were immediately on the spot, many of which could throw water more than a hundred feet high; but the noble firemen, to a man, of all the companies present, refused to throw one drop of water on the consuming building. All they did was to direct their engines to play upon the private buildings in the immediate vicinity of the blazing hall, some of which were in danger, as they were nearly joining the hall. . . . Such conduct in the Philadelphia fire companies deserves the highest praise and gratitude of all friends of the Union, and of all Southerners in particular; and I hope and trust the fire companies of New Orleans will hold a meeting, and testify in some suitable manner to the Philadelphia fire companies their sincere approbation of their noble conduct on this occasion."

Another Southerner wrote to a Georgian paper how he and a friend helped, and enjoyed the spectacle: —

"We lent our feeble efforts to effect the demolition of this castle of iniquity. . . . The fire companies repaired tardily to the scene of action, and not a drop of water did they pour upon that accursed Moloch until it was a heap of ruins. Sir! it would have gladdened your heart to have beheld that lofty tower of mischief enveloped in flames. The devouring element seemed to wear, combined with its terrible majesty, beauty and delight. To witness those beautiful spires of flame gave undoubted assurance to the heart of the Southron that in his brethren of the North he has friends."[1]

This shows what the mob discipline was. It did not drive Whittier from his non-resistant principles, as was the case with most of the men of that stamp who went nearly thirty years later to Kansas; it only made him more absolutely sure and resolute in proclaiming the antislavery gospel.

Nor was this the whole story. The next day a "Shelter for Coloured Orphans" was burned, and a church of the

[1] Linton's "Whittier," pp. 74-76.

coloured people attacked and damaged. The day before the first attack the Pennsylvania Antislavery Society had announced a meeting at the hall for the election of officers, and at the appointed hour it met by the smoking ruins and went through its business amid the howling of the mob. The tumults lasted a week, and at the end of this time the mayor offered a reward for the arrest of the rioters, from which nothing followed. The summary of the whole affair in the *Pennsylvania Freeman* was written by Whittier and Charles Burleigh. It was practically the record of the poet's baptism into the second degree of reform — the period of mob violence.

Years after, Whittier had a curious memorial of this period: —

"Once when he was passing through Portland, Me., a man, seeing him go by, stepped out of his shop and asked if his name were Whittier, and if he were not the man who was stoned, years ago, by a mob at Concord. The answer being in the affirmative, he said he believed a devil possessed him that night; for he had no reason to wish evil either to Whittier or Thompson, yet he was filled with a desire to kill them, and he thought he should have done so if they had not escaped. He added that the mob was like a crowd of demons, and he knew one man who had mixed a black dye to dip them [the abolitionists] in, which would be almost impossible to get off. He could not explain to himself or to another the state of mind he was in." [1]

[1] Fields's "Whittier," p. 47.

CHAPTER VI

A DIVISION IN THE RANKS

TIMES of peace, it is said, have few historians, but times of war have still fewer, because the hotter the fight the harder it is to stop and describe it. It will be useless to attempt any full explanation, for the readers of to-day, of the great division which embittered the lives of so many among the early abolitionists, as years passed on. The strength of character which makes a leader of reform is not easily combined with the sweet attributes of the peacemaker; and after the right to agitate a great principle is fought for and won, there is apt to be a good deal of further pugilism needed in determining just how it shall be agitated. The leader of the antislavery movement was of course Garrison, and he had been Whittier's especial guide and source of influence in his personal career; so that their mutual relation became in time a difficult question. After the *Liberator* had been mobbed into fame, it turned out to be in the hands of a man who had, not one moral aim alone in view, but many; who had a whole quiver full of arrows to discharge at a dozen public evils, and would by no means be limited by any one else in the right of selection. This was all very proper if Garrison's newspaper belonged to him in fee simple; but what became of it as an organ of the whole antislavery body, of which Whittier happened to be one?

There was the Bible question, the Sunday question, the labour question; all these were to be handled by a man who had in him far more of fighting capacity, of logical brain, than could be limited to one cause alone. On most of these points Whittier was as radical as Garrison, but he was by temperament more strictly executive, and wished to lay out the work systematically and fight each battle by itself. Then came the great question of voting or non-voting, and here Garrison's disunion attitude, in itself logical enough, went against Whittier's whole temperament; and it ended in their being, for a time at least, leaders and combatants in two separate armies. This involved some differences of attitude on very pressing questions; and the transfer of the other antislavery newspaper, the *Emancipator*, to the possession of those who could not wholly support Garrison, was an act which divided families and left seeds of bitterness of which the "Life of Garrison" by his sons gives a thorough and laborious record. It would now lead into a labyrinth were I to follow it up; it is enough to say that Mrs. Chapman's view as to Whittier — so the latter himself told me at one time — was this, "As to that, the only question is, whether Whittier is more knave or fool." Now Mrs. Chapman was, as I have already said, as distinctly the leader among the antislavery women as was Garrison among the men.

In short, the question of union or disunion drew a sharp line of cleavage among those already enlisted, and it was impossible, I suppose, for the originators of the whole movement to do otherwise than they did

— this outcome involving, it must be owned, much bitter quarrelling. But I am glad to testify, for the credit of all concerned, that upon the younger men who came on the stage after the lines were first drawn, there was imposed no necessity of taking sides; and I never, for one, found any difficulty in working with both bodies of men and women — the Garrisonians or Disunionists and the voting abolitionists or Liberty Party men. The latter, it must be remembered, was the organisation which became the "Free Soil" party, then the "Republican" party, and in that form finally controlled the nation. It must be owned, however, in viewing the attitude of these two dividing factions, that the Disunionists were in general the more interesting class personally and more eloquent in speech than their voting brethren, precisely because they could speak without the slightest reference to policy or organisation; that the very leaders of the latter, such as Whittier and Samuel E. Sewall, happened to have no gift of platform eloquence, though much faculty of organising and conciliating; that the very fact of the entanglement of voting abolitionists with party leaders who never thoroughly belonged with them, such as Clay and Van Buren, was an embarrassment and a hindrance; and finally, that the immense and unflinching weight of the women, as non-voters, was thrown on the side of Garrison and his party, whereas the voting abolitionists were often tempted to keep rather shy of a non-voting sex. All this I say, although observation has taught me that all these differences of policy, which seemed such a life-and-death matter at the time, are now as uninteresting to the younger generation as is antimasonry or any other cause which once shook the nation. It is, moreover, the actual fact that though the leaders such as Garrison and Whittier opposed and distrusted each other for a time, they ended after many years in renewed friendship: just as Adams and Jefferson, after years of far bitterer contest, could spend their old age in the friendliest correspondence, and even death found them in such a hand-and-hand relation that it took them both on the same day, and that day the anniversary of the Declaration of Independence.

In the meanwhile, each of the abolitionist leaders followed the path that belonged to his temperament. Garrison had no gift for personal organisation, in the politician's sense; but no man ever excelled him in the strength and fearlessness of his individual statements, The clear maxims of his early platform, "I will not equivocate, I will not apologise, I will not retreat a single inch, and I will be heard," simply marked him as one of the most absolutely straightforward hitters who ever encountered a great wrong. Hence came his power; while Whittier, equally sincere, proved to have, unlike Garrison, an unexpected tact and skill of management; he could deal with professional politicians like Clay and Cushing; he could adapt himself to their limitations, and show cause why they should be on his side. Even after he knew them to be worthless for freedom, but had need of them, he would keep them in his power to the last. One secret of this was his absolute unselfishness; a thing in which he surpassed even Garrison, who possessed the love of power, after all, though in its most high-minded form, and was never quite at ease in a secondary position; whereas such an attitude never troubled Whittier at all. This is clearly set forth in a letter to the latter's friend, Elizabeth Neall. The letter shows also that his sympathies as a consistent member of the Society of Friends went forth to the women speakers, whom he was criticised as not fully sustaining. After all, it is always a thing which depends on the individual temperament of reformers, how far they are to make use of a multiplex lens, and how far to concentrate all observation on a single point.

"To Elizabeth Neal.

"1839.

"For myself, abolition has been to me its own 'exceeding great reward.' It has repaid every sacrifice of time, of money, of reputation, of health, of ease, with the answer of a good conscience, and the happiness which grows out of benevolent exertions for the welfare of others. It has led me to examine myself. It has given me the acquaintance of some of the noblest and best of men and women. *It owes me nothing.* So, then, two of the youngest members of the Women's Society are to hold forth. . . . Shade of the Apostle Paul! What is this world coming to? Never mind, 'I like it hugely,' as Tristram Shandy said of Yorick's sermon, and would like it better to see them wield in their delicate fingers the thunderbolts of abolition oratory. As the author of 'John Gilpin' said of the hero and his horse:—

'And when he next doth ride abroad,
May I be there to see!'

Seriously, I see no good reason why they should not speak as well as their elders. 'Let the daughters prophesy,' agreeably to the promise of the prophet Joel, and let the doors be thrown open to all without distinction of sex, and then another part of the promise will be verified, 'the young men shall see visions!' I go the whole length as regards the rights of women, however, although I sometimes joke a little about it. I am afraid it is a besetting sin of mine to do so in reference to many things in which I feel a sober and real interest. I have repented of it a thousand times, especially as it gave those who were not intimately acquainted with me a false idea of my character. . . ."[1]

The only record in the "Life of Garrison" by his sons — perhaps the most thoroughly executed biography ever written in America, though it could hardly be expected to be the most absolutely impartial — of any final interview showing the cleavage between him and Whittier is in a letter from Lucretia Mott, written on Feb. 25, 1852. She says: "Maria W. Chapman wrote me that he [Whittier] was in the [antislavery] office a few months since, bemoaning to Garrison that there should have been any divisions. 'Why could we not all go on together?' 'Why not, indeed?' said Garrison; '*we* stand just where we did. I see no reason why you cannot coöperate with the American Society.' 'Oh,' replied Whittier, 'but the American Society is not what it once was. It has the coat, the hat, and the waistcoat of the old society, but the life has passed out of it.' 'Are you not ashamed,' said Garrison, 'to come here wondering why we cannot go on together? No wonder you can't coöperate with a suit of old clothes.'"[2]

How far Garrison did justice to the real strength of Whittier's nature will perhaps always remain somewhat doubtful, in view of the fact that eight years before this, in 1834, he had briefly characterised him as "highly poetical, exuberant, and beautiful."[3] It is possible he may have been rather surprised, in later years, to find his young proselyte developing a will of

[1] Pickard, I. 218–19. [2] "Garrison's Life," III. 35.
[3] "Garrison's Life," I. 461.

his own. There was certainly a phase of detached relations, when Whittier freely endorsed the prevalent criticism of Garrison as dictatorial; and when Garrison's foremost counsellor among antislavery women Mrs. Chapman, used the phrases she employed about Whittier. But it is needless to explore these little divergences of the saints, and it is certain that Garrison, at the thirtieth anniversary of the founding of the American Antislavery Society, spoke of Whittier as "known and honoured throughout the civilised world." He added: "I have no words to express my sense of the value of his services. There are few living who have done so much to operate upon the public mind and conscience and heart of our country for the abolition of slavery as John Greenleaf Whittier."

Whittier, in his letter, made this companion tribute to Garrison: —

"I must not close this letter without confessing that I cannot be sufficiently thankful to the Divine Providence which, in a great measure through thy instrumentality, turned me so early away from what Roger Williams calls 'the world's great trinity, pleasure, profit, and honour,' to take side with the poor and oppressed. I am not insensible to literary reputation; I love, perhaps too well, the praise and good will of my fellow-men; but I set a higher value on my name as appended to the Antislavery Declaration of 1833 than on the title-page of any book. Looking over a life marked by many errors and shortcomings, I rejoice that I have been able to maintain the pledge of that signature."

The lesson thus conveyed is so fine that I linger further upon it, to give some extracts from Whittier's own review of the matter in his introduction to Oliver Johnson's "William Lloyd Garrison and his Times."

"I do not know that any word of mine can give additional interest to this memorial of William Lloyd Garrison from the pen of one of his earliest and most devoted friends, whose privilege it has been to share his confidence and his labours for nearly half a century: but I cannot well forego the opportunity afforded me to add briefly my testimony to the tribute to the memory of the great Reformer, whose friendship I have shared, and with whom I have been associated in a common cause from youth to age.

"My acquaintance with him commenced in boyhood. My father was a subscriber to his first paper, the *Free Press*, and the humanitarian tone of his editorials awakened a deep interest in our little household, which was increased by a visit which he made us. When he afterwards edited the *Journal of the Times*, at Bennington, Vt., I ventured to write him a letter of encouragement and sympathy, urging him to continue his labours against slavery, and assuring him that he could 'do great things,' an unconscious prophecy which has been fulfilled beyond the dream of my boyish enthusiasm. The friendship thus commenced has remained unbroken through half a century, confirming my early confidence in his zeal and devotion, and in the great intellectual and moral strength which he brought to the cause with which his name is identified.

"During the long and hard struggle in which the abolitionists were engaged, and amidst the new and difficult questions and side issues which presented themselves, it could scarcely be otherwise than that differences of opinion and action should arise among them. The leader and his disciples could not always see alike. My friend, the author of this book, I think, generally found himself in full accord with him, while I often decidedly dissented. I felt it my duty to use my right of citizenship at the ballot-box in the cause of liberty, while Garrison, with equal sincerity, judged and counselled otherwise. Each acted under a sense of individual duty and responsibility, and our personal relations were undisturbed. If, at times, the great antislavery leader failed to do justice to the motives of those who, while in hearty sympathy with his hatred of slavery, did not agree with some of his opinions and methods, it was but the pardonable and not unnatural result of his intensity of purpose and his self-identification with the cause he advocated; and, while compelled to dissent, in some particulars, from his judgment of men and measures, the great mass of the antislavery people recognised his moral leadership. The controversies of old and new organisation, non-resistance and political action, may now be looked upon by the parties to them who still survive, with the philosophic calmness which follows the subsidence of prejudice and passion. We were but fallible men, and doubtless often erred in feeling, speech, and action. Ours was but the common experience of reformers in all ages.

"'Never in Custom's oilèd grooves
The world to a higher level moves,
But grates and grinds with friction hard
On granite boulder and flinty shard.
Ever the Virtues blush to find
The Vices wearing their badge behind,
And Graces and Charities feel the fire
Wherein the sins of the age expire.'

"It is too late now to dwell on these differences. I choose rather, with a feeling of gratitude to God, to recall the great happiness of labouring with the noble company of whom Garrison was the central figure. I love to think of him as he seemed to me, when in the fresh dawn of manhood he sat with me in the old Haverhill farmhouse, revolving even then schemes of benevolence; or, with cheery smile, welcoming me to his frugal meal of bread and milk in the dingy Boston printing-room; or, as I found him in the gray December morning in the small attic of a coloured man, in Philadelphia, finishing his night-long task of drafting his immortal *Declaration of Sentiments* of the American Antislavery Society; or, as I saw him in the jail of Leverett Street, after his almost miraculous escape from the mob, playfully inviting me to share the safe lodgings which the state had provided for him: and in all the varied scenes and situations where we acted together our parts in the great endeavour and success of Freedom.

"The verdict of posterity in his case may be safely anticipated. With the true reformers and benefactors of his race he occupies a place inferior to none other. The private lives of many who fought well the battles of humanity have not been without spot or blemish. But his private character, like his public, knew no dishonour. No shadow of suspicion rests upon the white statue of a life, the fitting garland of which should be the Alpine flower that symbolises noble purity."[1]

It is nevertheless to be observed that it became necessary for Whittier, more than once, in the antislavery movement, to dissent widely from Garrison and his more immediate circle in regard to those reformers who worked on a somewhat different plane. It is a fact worth noticing, for instance, because very characteristic, that Whittier, like that very able woman, Mrs. Lydia Maria Child, always differed from Garrison and his more intimate followers in the view they took of the Rev. Dr. William Ellery Channing, to whom Whittier had written, of his own impulse, in early youth, a serious appeal urging him to enter strenuously upon the antislavery agitation. Whittier was, it must be remembered, addressing one incomparably his superior at that time, in prominence and influence, as in years. It was a bold letter to be written by a shy Quaker youth of twenty-six to a man more than twice his years, for Channing was then almost fifty-four. A yet unknown man, Whittier was offering counsel to the most popular clergyman in Boston. Written in 1834, the letter long preceded Channing's Faneuil Hall speech of 1837, which first clearly committed him to

[1] "Works," pp. 189–92.

the antislavery movement; and it still farther preceded his work on slavery in 1841, which identified him with the enterprise and made him, in the minds of the more moderate, its recognised leader. The fact is the more interesting, inasmuch as Channing himself, in spite of his vast influence with a class whom Garrison had as yet scarcely touched, was always regarded with distrust, almost with hostility, by the abolitionists proper, and was denounced by Mrs. Maria Weston Chapman, as one who "had neither insight, courage, nor firmness." Whittier, on the other hand, always maintained, that after Mrs. Child, Dr. Channing had made greater sacrifices for the antislavery cause than any one, in view of the height and breadth of his previous influence and popularity.[1]

In November, 1837, a small volume of Whittier's poems was issued in Boston by the publisher of the *Liberator*, Isaac Knapp. It was first printed without consulting the poet himself, and was entitled, "Poems written during the Progress of the Abolition Question in the United States, between the years 1830 and 1838, by John G. Whittier." This was the first edition of his works; but the first authorised edition did not appear until a year later, in November, when a small volume, entitled simply "Poems," was issued by Joseph Healy, financial agent of the Philadelphia Society. This consisted of one hundred and eighty pages, and was not limited to his antislavery verse; including fifty poems in all, only eleven of which are retained in the permanent edition of his works. The little book is ennobled by one of Coleridge's finest passages, used as a motto, as follows: —

[1] The letter addressed to him may be found in Pickard's "Whittier," I. 137.

"'There is a time to keep silence,' saith Solomon. But when I proceeded to the first verse of the fourth chapter of the Ecclesiastes, 'and considered all the oppressions that are done under the sun, and beheld the tears of such as are oppressed, and they have had no comforter; and on the side of the oppressors there was power,' I concluded this was *not* the time to keep silence; for Truth should be spoken at all times, but more especially at those times when to speak Truth is dangerous."

In 1840 Whittier's health had become impaired anew; his father had died, and his mother, sister, and aunt had removed their residence to Amesbury—partly for the sake of nearness to their meeting-house; and he joined them there and made the house his legal domicile, as it is now his memorial home.

His service to freedom, after ill health had driven him from Philadelphia, was irregular in place and form, but constant. He passed from Amesbury to Boston and thence to New York, to Saratoga, to Albany, and to western Pennsylvania, and wherever there was to be an antislavery convention; which meant, in his case, a convention based upon the ballot, aiming at political action, and still holding to the faint hope that Henry Clay might yet become its leader, and that Caleb Cushing might espouse its cause. At one time Whittier and Henry B. Stanton were deputed by the American Antislavery Society to go through Pennsylvania and find, if they could, seventy public speakers who would take part in the war against slavery.[1] He had at one time planned, when he felt himself more in command of his bodily forces, to attend the World's Antislavery Convention at London (June, 1840), but being cautioned by the well-known

[1] Pickard's "Whittier," I. 250.

physician, Dr. Henry I. Bowditch, he forebore to take the risk, his heart being at that period the point of danger.

Of the later tests which came to abolitionists and sometimes separated them into opposing ranks, little need be said, for Whittier was never personally combative, and though he was severely tested as to his peace principles, yet the Quaker principle carried him safely through. When I was in Kansas in 1856, in the times of trouble, I could hear of but one of the theoretical non-resistants who had gone thither and who had adhered faithfully to his principles. I did not agree with these views, but went out of my way to call upon him and express my respect, a feeling I could not quite entertain for those who had backslidden, and could then give as an excuse that they "never imagined there could be such people in the world as the Border Ruffians." With all Whittier's Arab look and his admiration of General Gordon, I think he would have found himself exposed to being lynched and yet have been a Quaker still; just as his old friend Garrison, through all the fugitive slave cases in Boston, kept steadfastly at his desk, regarding these as mere incidents, and the punctuality of the next issue of the *Liberator* as the important thing. When it came to the still more difficult test of John Brown, this letter to Mrs. Child showed Whittier to be the non-resistant still: —

"OCTOBER 21st, [1859].

"MY DEAR FRIEND, — I was glad to get a line from thee, and glad of the opportunity it affords me and my sister to express our admiration of thy generous sympathy with the brave but, methinks, sadly misguided Captain Brown. We feel deeply (who does not?) for the noble-hearted, self-sacrificing old man. But as friends of peace, as well as believers in the Sermon on the Mount, we dare not lend *any* countenance to such attempts as that at Harper's Ferry.

"I hope, in our admiration of the noble traits of John Brown's character, we shall be careful how we encourage a repetition of his rash and ill-judged movement. Thou and I believe in 'a more excellent way.' I have just been looking at one of the *pikes* sent here by a friend in Baltimore. It is not a Christian weapon; it looks too much like murder.

"God is now putting our non-resistance principles to a severe test. I hope we shall not give the lie to our life-long professions. I quite agree with thee that we must judge of Brown by *his* standards; but at the same time we must be true to our settled convictions, and to the duty we owe to humanity.

"Thou wilt see how difficult it is for me to write as thou request. My heart is too heavy and sorrowful. I cannot write now, and can only *wait*, with fervent prayer that the cause we love may receive no detriment."

CHAPTER VII

WHITTIER AS A SOCIAL REFORMER

It must be borne in mind, as regards Whittier, that he lived not merely at a time when the direct question of human freedom was uppermost, but in a period when all questions of religious freedom and of social reorganisation were coming to the front in many ways. In some of these directions, real progress came out of such agitations, and at the very least they kept before the public the need of perpetual change and rearrangement of laws and usages, to keep up with the progress of invention and of democratic institutions. It was a time when Emerson wrote of the social structure, "The nobles shall not any longer, as feudal lords, have power of life and death over the churls, but now in another shape, as capitalists, shall in all love and peace eat these up as before."[1]

It was not possible for Whittier, with his temperament and principles, to keep himself aloof from these seething agitations; and he showed both the courage of Quakerism and its guarded moderation in encountering the new problems and their advocates. This is visible, for instance, in such letters as the following: —

[1] Emerson, "Life and Letters in New England."

"To ANN E. WENDELL.

"LYNN, 11th mo., 1840.

"I was in Boston this week, and looked in twice upon the queer gathering of heterogeneous spirits at the Chardon Street chapel assembled under a call issued by Maria W. Chapman, Abby Kelley, and others, to discuss the subjects of the Sabbath, ministry, and church organisations, and some twenty other collateral subjects. When I was present the chapel was crowded, a motley-opinioned company, from the Calvinist of the straitest sect to the infidel and scoffer. Half of the forenoon of the first day was spent in debating whether the convention should be organised by the choice of president and secretary, or whether these old-fashioned restraints should be set aside as unworthy of advocates of 'the largest liberty,' leaving each member to do and say what seemed right in his own eyes! It was finally decided to have a president. Then came on a discussion about the Sabbath, in which Garrison and two transcendental Unitarians, and a woman by the name of Folsom, argued that every day should be held sacred; that it was not a rest from labour but from sin that was wanted; that keeping First day as holy was not required, etc. On the other hand, Amos A. Phelps, Dr. Osgood, and some others contended for the Calvinistic and generally received views of the subject. Dr. Channing, John Pierpont, and many other distinguished men were present, but took no part in the discussions. No Friends were members of the convention, although there were several lookers-on. Judging from the little I saw and heard, I do not think the world will be much the wiser for the debate. It may have a tendency to unsettle some minds."[1]

It was in connection with "The Tent on the Beach" that Whittier printed in the New York *Nation* what is perhaps the best statement of the comparative position which poetry and practical reform held in his life. It is as follows: —

[1] Pickard, I. 266–67.

"I am very well aware that merely personal explanations are not likely to be as interesting to the public as to the parties concerned; but I am induced to notice what is either a misconception on thy part, or as is most probable, a failure on my own to make myself clearly understood. In the review of 'The Tent on the Beach,' in thy paper of last week, I confess I was not a little surprised to find myself represented as regretting my lifelong and active participation in the great conflict which has ended in the emancipation of the slave, and that I had not devoted myself to merely literary pursuits. In the half-playful lines upon which this statement is founded, if I did not feel at liberty to boast of my antislavery labours and magnify my editorial profession, I certainly did not mean to underrate them, or express the shadow of a regret that they had occupied so large a share of my time and thought. The simple fact is, that I cannot be sufficiently thankful to the Divine Providence that so early called my attention to the great interests of humanity, saving me from the poor ambitions and miserable jealousies of a selfish pursuit of literary reputation. Up to a comparatively recent period, my writings have been simply episodical, something apart from the real object and aim of my life; and whatever of favour they have found with the public has come to me as a grateful surprise, rather than as an expected reward. As I have never staked all on the chances of authorship, I have been spared the pain of disappointment and the temptation to envy those, who, as men of letters, deservedly occupy a higher place in the popular estimation than I have ever aspired to.

"Truly your friend,

"JOHN G. WHITTIER.

"Amesbury, 9th, 3d mo., 1867."

It is known that in the same conscientious spirit he was unwilling to insert in his "Songs of Three Centuries" Mrs. Howe's "Battle Hymn of the Republic," but as he wrote to his assistant editor, "I got over my Quaker scruples, or rather stifled them, and put in the 'Battle Hymn.'" He adds that he cannot do justice to Campbell's works in this series, "but we can't print his war pieces, and so we will let him slide."

One of his points of prominence was naturally his position as a member of the Society of Friends. On the publication of the extended "Memorial History of Boston," in four large volumes, in 1880, edited by the unquestioned chief among Massachusetts historians, Justin Winsor, Whittier furnished by request a poem bearing on early local history, "The King's Missive." The first verse of the poem, now well known, was as follows:—

> "Under the great hill sloping bare
> To cove and meadow and Common lot,
> In his council chamber and oaken chair,
> Sat the worshipful Governor Endicott.
> A grave, strong man who knew no peer
> In the pilgrim land, where he ruled in fear
> Of God, not man, and for good or ill
> He held his trust with an iron will."

To this poem a reply was written by the Rev. G. E. Ellis, president of the Massachusetts Historical Society, questioning its statement of facts. This led to some discussion between him and the author, and Whittier wrote in reply the only long prose statement, I believe, which was drawn from him, in a polemic way, after his early antislavery pamphlets. The Massachusetts Historical Society afterward put, in a manner, its seal of acceptance on this, when it chose Whittier as a member; and I think that it was generally admitted among its members that Dr. Ellis went rather too far in his attempt to vindicate the character of the Puritans for justice or moderation. Whittier himself, in reprinting the poem in his collected works, adds, tranquilly, "The publication of the ballad led to some discussion as to the historical truthfulness of the picture, but I have seen no reason to rub out any of the figures, or alter the lines and colours."[1]

As this controversy tested Whittier in an important light, I give a specimen passage from his argument; and all the more because he did not include it in his permanent collection of prose works, partly perhaps from its character of personal antagonism, which he so greatly disliked. He says: —

"Nor can it be said that the persecution grew out of the 'intrusion,' 'indecency,' and 'effrontery' of the persecuted.

"It owed its origin to the settled purpose of the ministers and leading men of the colony to permit no difference of opinion on religious matters. They had banished the Baptists, and whipped at least one of them. They had hunted down Gorton and his adherents; they had imprisoned Dr. Child, an Episcopalian, for petitioning the General Court for toleration. They had driven some of their best citizens out of their jurisdiction, with Anne Hutchinson, and the gifted minister, Wheelwright. Any dissent on the part of their own fellow-citizens was punished as severely as the heresy of strangers.

"The charge of 'indecency' comes with ill grace from the authorities of the Massachusetts Colony. The first Quakers who arrived in Boston, Ann Austin and Mary Fisher, were arrested on board the ship before landing, their books taken from them and burned by the constable, and they themselves brought before Deputy Governor Bellingham, in the absence of Endicott. This astute magistrate ordered them to be *stripped naked and their bodies to be carefully examined, to see if there was not the Devil's mark on them as witches.* They were then sent to jail, their cell window was boarded up, and they were left without food or light, until the master

[1] "Works," I. 381.

of the vessel that brought them was ordered to take them to Barbadoes. When Endicott returned he thought they had been treated too leniently, and declared that he would have had them whipped.

"After this, almost every town in the province was favoured with the spectacle of aged and young women stripped to the middle, tied to a cart-tail, and dragged through the streets and scourged without mercy by the constable's whip. It is not strange that these atrocious proceedings, in two or three instances, unsettled the minds of the victims. Lydia Wardwell of Hampton, who, with her husband, had been reduced to almost total destitution by persecution, was summoned by the church of which she had been a member to appear before it to answer to the charge of non-attendance. She obeyed the call by appearing in the unclothed condition of the sufferers whom she had seen under the constable's whip. For this she was taken to Ipswich and stripped to the waist, tied to a rough post, which tore her bosom as she writhed under the lash, and severely scourged to the satisfaction of a crowd of lookers-on at the tavern. One, and only one, other instance is adduced in the person of Deborah Wilson of Salem. She had seen her friends and neighbours scourged naked through the street, among them her brother, who was banished on pain of death. She, like all Puritans, had been educated in the belief of the plenary inspiration of Scripture, and had brooded over the strange 'signs' and testimonies of the Hebrew prophets. It seemed to her that the time had arrived for some similar demonstration, and that it was her duty to walk abroad in the disrobed condition to which her friends had been subjected, as a sign and warning to the persecutors. Whatever of 'indecency' there was in these cases was directly chargeable upon the atrocious persecution. At the door of the magistrates and ministers of Massachusetts must be laid the insanity of the conduct of these unfortunate women.

"But Boston, at least, had no voluntary Godivas. The only disrobed women in its streets were made so by Puritan sheriffs and constables, who dragged them amidst jeering crowds at the cart-tail, stripped for the lash, which in one instance laid open with a ghastly gash the bosom of a young mother!"[1]

It has been stated that Mr. Whittier at one time expressed to a member of the Massachusetts Historical Society his intention to prepare a full and exhaustive history of the relation of Puritan and Quaker in the seventeenth century, but there seems no evidence that he followed up this project.

There was undoubtedly in Whittier, amid all his quietness of life, that impulsiveness which revealed itself in his brilliant eye and subdued decision of manner. "A good deal has been said," as Mr. Robert S. Rantoul has admirably pointed out, "about Mr. Whittier's fighting blood; whether it came from Huguenot or Norman veins, or from his Indian-fighting ancestors who deserted the 'meeting' for the trail and camp. He had a good deal of the natural man left under his brown homespun, waistcoat, and straight collar. He had the reticence and presence of an Arab chief, with the eye of an eagle." Among all Howells's characters in fiction, the one who most caught Whittier's fancy was "that indomitable old German, Linden," in the "Hazard of New Fortunes," whom he characterised, in writing to Mrs. Fields, as "that saint of the rather godless sect of dynamiters and atheists — a grand figure."

Besides the general spirit of freedom which Whittier imbibed with his Quaker blood and training, he had also in his blood the instincts of labour, which tended to the elevation of the labouring class. This I know well, for I lent a hand, when living in the next town, to an agitation for the Ten Hour Bill at Amesbury, and there are various

[1] Kennedy's "Whittier," 275–79.

references to it in his brief letters to me. A natural politician of the higher sort, he rejoiced in an effort to bring such a bill before the state legislature, where it finally triumphed. Thus I find a letter, probably written in 1848, but imperfectly dated, as his letters often were: —

"AMESBURY, 13th, 7th mo."

"MY DEAR HIGGINSON:

"Thy letter was clearly to the purpose and was read at the Levee, and will be published this week in the *Villager:* — Thou will see by the *Villager* of last week what we are doing about the Ten Hour Law. That must be a point in our elections this fall — I think we can carry it through the next legislature.

I hope thou will be able to go to the Dist. Convention at Lowell tomorrow. Our del. is instructed to go for thee as one of the delegates to Pittsburg. Don't refuse. We shall be glad to see thee at any time.

"Ever thine,"
"J. G. W."

On application to the Hon. George W. Cate, he has refreshed my memory in regard to the details of the strike which led to this ten-hour agitation, and they are as follows: —

"Your memory of Mr. Whittier's position in regard to strikes is correct. At the time of the *Derby* 'turnout, or strike,' at Amesbury, which was many years ago, in '52 I think, Mr. Whittier was in full sympathy with the strikers. I think the particulars of the turnout were given quite fully by C. D. Wright. At that time, all the people who were employed in the mills were a very intelligent class of operatives, and natives. All took a deep interest in their work. It had for many years been their custom to go into the mill early and to come out for a few minutes at about ten o'clock A.M., and order their dinner and get a luncheon. The habit had been in existence for years, and had become an unwritten law with the operatives. Agent Derby denied them these privileges, and they refused to return to work. The result of this disagreement terminated in the old operatives leaving, and in the employment of a large number of foreigners, which entirely changed the character of the operatives in Amesbury."[1]

So in regard to spiritual liberty Whittier addressed a poem in indignation to Pius IX. after his acceptance of the French aid against his own people, but he added in a note: —

"The writer of these lines is no enemy of Catholics. He has, on more than one occasion, exposed himself to the censures of his Protestant brethren, by his strenuous endeavours to procure indemnification for the owners of the convent destroyed near Boston. He defended the cause of the Irish patriots long before it had become popular in this country; and he was one of the first to urge the most liberal aid to the suffering and starving population of the Catholic island. The severity of his language finds its ample apology in the reluctant confession of one of the most eminent Romish priests, the eloquent and devoted Father Ventura."

And he added a similar reproach in "The Prisoners at Naples," and in "The Peace of Europe, 1852."

As to the temperance movement, it seems a little amusing to find Whittier taking for the theme of his first prose newspaper article, "Robert Burns," and for his second subject, on the following week, "Temperance." These appeared in the Haverhill *Gazette*, the editor of which, Mr. Thayer, father of the late Professor James B. Thayer, of the Harvard Law School, was one of the earliest American editors to take up this theme. A

[1] Ms. Letter, Aug. 26, 1902.

year later Whittier writes from Amesbury, whither he had removed: "I have one item of good news from Haverhill. The old distillery has had its fires quenched at last. C. has sold out, and the building is to be converted into stores." Whittier himself, as I remember well, at Atlantic Club dinners, was one of the few who took no wine among that group of authors.

The attitude of Whittier toward reform agitations in general was never better shown than in his prompt response to the announcement of certain limitations placed by George Peabody on the church built largely by his money in Georgetown, Mass. The facts were first brought to light by the New York *Independent* on Jan. 16, 1868, by the following statement: —

"*A Marred Memorial.* — Mr. George Peabody, the banker, gave money for the erection of the Memorial Church in Georgetown, Mass., the town of his birth. The church was dedicated on the 8th of January, with interesting exercises, one of the striking features of which was the singing of the following hymn, written for the occasion by John G. Whittier. . . . We venture to say that if the poet had known the conditions which the banker saw fit to impose on the Memorial Church, the poem would never have been written, and its author's name would never have been lent to the occasion. A correspondent of the *Independent* writes: 'Mr. Peabody says in his letter that the church shall never be used for any lectures, discussions of political subjects, or other matters inconsistent with the gospel. I do not give his precise words, but this is the substance. The church will be deeded to the society on the express condition that neither Liberty nor Temperance, nor any other subject of Reform, shall ever be introduced into the pulpit.'"

Mr. Whittier published a card in the Boston *Transcript* of Jan. 30, as follows: —

"In writing the 'Hymn for the Memorial Church at Georgetown,' the author, as his verses indicate, has sole reference to the tribute of a brother and sister to the memory of a departed mother, — a tribute which seemed and still seems to him, in itself considered, very beautiful and appropriate; but he has since seen, with surprise and sorrow, a letter read at the dedication, imposing certain extraordinary restrictions upon the society which is to occupy the house. It is due to himself, as a simple act of justice, to say that had he known of the existence of that letter previously, the hymn would never have been written, nor his name in any way connected with the proceedings."

To Whittier, as to many, including all advocates of universal peace, the results of the Civil War brought some misgivings, through the means by which they were attained. He wrote thus to the woman who had first brought the antislavery movement into American literature: —

"To Lydia Maria Child.

"1875.

"Thy confession as respects thy services in the cause of freedom and emancipation does not shock me at all. The emancipation that came by military necessity and enforced by bayonets was not the emancipation for which we worked and prayed. But, like the Apostle, I am glad the gospel of Freedom was preached, even if by strife and emulation. It cannot be said that we did it; we, indeed, had no triumph. But the work itself was a success. It made us stronger and better men and women. Some had little to sacrifice, but I always felt, my dear friend, that thee had made the costliest offering to the cause. For thee alone, of all of us, had won a literary reputation which any one might have been proud of. I read all thy early work with enthusiastic interest, as I have all the later. Some time ago I searched Boston and New York for thy 'Hobomok,' and succeeded in finding a defaced copy. How few American books can compare with thy 'Philothea'! Why, my friend, thy reputation, in spite of the antislavery surrender of it for so many years, is still a living and beautiful reality. And after all, good as thy books are, we know thee to be better than any book. I wish thee could know how proudly and tenderly thee is loved and honoured by the best and wisest of the land."[1]

Whittier was the only one of his immediate literary circle, except Fields the publisher, who unequivocally supported woman suffrage from the beginning of the agitation. It was of course easier for members of the Society of Friends to do this than for others, yet many Friends opposed it, even vehemently. He wrote as early as 1839, "I go the whole length as regards the rights of women"; and he wrote again to the Woman's Suffrage Convention at Worcester, in 1850: —

"Come what may, Nature is inexorable; she will reverse none of her laws at the bidding of male or female conventions; and men and women, with or without the right of suffrage, will continue to be men and women still. In the event of the repeal of certain ungenerous, not to say unmanly, enactments, limiting and abridging the rights and privileges of women, we may safely confide in the adaptive powers of Nature. She will take care of the new fact in her own way, and reconcile it to the old, through the operation of her attractive or repellent forces. Let us, then, not be afraid to listen to the claims and demands of those who, in some sort at least, represent the feelings and interests of those nearest and dearest to us. Let Oliver ask for more. It is scarcely consistent with our assumed superiority to imitate the horror and wide-orbed consternation of Mr. Bumble and his parochial associates, on a similar occasion."

[1] Pickard's "Whittier," II. 603–04.

Later, when the movement had got farther on, and he was invited to a convention on the subject, held at Newport, R.I., on Aug. 25, 1869, he replied thus explicitly and also wisely: —

"AMESBURY, MASS., 12th, 8th Month, 1869.

"I have received thy letter inviting me to attend the Convention in behalf of Woman's Suffrage, at Newport, R.I., on the 25th inst. I do not see how it is possible for me to accept the invitation; and, were I to do so, the state of my health would prevent me from taking such a part in the meeting as would relieve me from the responsibility of seeming to sanction anything in its action which might conflict with my own views of duty or policy. Yet I should do myself great injustice if I did not embrace this occasion to express my general sympathy with the movement. I have seen no good reason why mothers, wives, and daughters should not have the same right of person, property, and citizenship which fathers, husbands, and brothers have.

"The sacred memory of mother and sister; the wisdom and dignity of women of my own religious communion who have been accustomed to something like equality in rights as well as duties; my experience as a co-worker with noble and self-sacrificing women, as graceful and helpful in their household duties as firm and courageous in their public advocacy of unpopular truth; the steady friendships which have inspired and strengthened me, and the reverence and respect which I feel for human nature, irrespective of sex, — compel me to look with something more than acquiescence on the efforts you are making. I frankly confess that I am not able to foresee all the consequences of the great social and political change proposed, but of this I am, at least, sure, it is always safe to do right, and the truest expediency is simple justice. I can understand, without sharing, the misgivings of those who fear that, when the vote drops from woman's hand into the ballot-box, the beauty and sentiment, the bloom and sweetness, of womankind will go with it. But in this matter it seems to me that we can trust Nature. Stronger than statutes or conventions, she will be conservative of all that the true man loves and honours in woman. Here and there may be found an equivocal, unsexed Chevalier d'Eon, but the eternal order and fitness of things will remain. I have no fear that man will be less manly or woman less womanly when they meet on terms of equality before the law.

"On the other hand, I do not see that the exercise of the ballot by woman will prove a remedy for all the evils of which she justly complains. It is her right as truly as mine, and when she asks for it, it is something less than manhood to withhold it. But, unsupported by a more practical education, higher aims, and a deeper sense of the responsibilities of life and duty, it is not likely to prove a blessing in her hands any more than in man's.

"With great respect and hearty sympathy, I am very truly thy friend."

Again he wrote, of a speech by that eminently clear-headed and able woman, Miss Alice Freeman, now Mrs. G. H. Palmer:—

"AMESBURY, 7th mo., 1881.

"Miss Freeman's speech was eloquent and wise — the best thing in the Institute. Perhaps even Francis Parkman might think she could be safely trusted to vote."

These opinions, it will be seen, cover an interval of nearly half a century.

CHAPTER VIII

PERSONAL QUALITIES

THAT acute, if not always impartial, observer, Mr. George W. Smalley, says of the most famous of modern English Quakers, John Bright, "There was no courtlier person than this Quaker, none whose manners were more perfect. . . . If there had been no standard of good manners, he would have created one. . . . Swift said, 'Whosoever makes the fewest persons uneasy is the best-bred man in the company.'"[1]

Tried by this last standard, at least, Whittier was unsurpassed; and living in America, where artificial standards are at least secondary, he never found himself misplaced. The relation between himself and others rested wholly on real grounds, and could be more easily computed. Personally I met him first in 1843, when the excitement of the "Latimer case" still echoed through Massachusetts, and the younger abolitionists, of whom I was one, were full of the joy of eventful living. I was then nineteen, and saw the poet for the first time at an eating-house known as Campbell's, and then quite a resort for reformers of all sorts, and incidentally of economical college students. Some one near me said, "There is Whittier." I saw before me a man of striking personal appearance; tall, slender, with olive complexion, black hair, straight,

[1] "London Letters," I. 124.

black eyebrows, brilliant eyes and an Oriental, Semitic cast of countenance. This was Whittier at thirty-five. Appetite vanished, and I resolved to speak to him, then or never. I watched till he rose from the table; and then advancing, said with boyish enthusiasm and, I doubt not, with boyish awkwardness also, "I should like to shake hands with the author of 'Massachusetts to Virginia.'" The poet, who was then, as always, one of the shyest of men, looked up as if frightened, then broke into a kindly smile, and said briefly, "Thy name, friend?" I gave it, we shook hands, and that was all; but to me it was like touching a hero's shield; and though I have since learned to count the friendship of Whittier as one of the great privileges of my life, yet nothing has ever displaced the recollection of that first boyish interview.

In comparing his whole life with that of his early friend Garrison, one must observe the fact that, while there was but a slight difference in their ages, Garrison was at first the leader, Whittier the follower. On the other hand, we notice that differences of temperament soon showed themselves and told both upon their careers and their memories. Partly as a result of this, each had a certain advantage with a later generation. Whittier, for instance, was childless; while Garrison left behind him a family of children to carry on his unfinished work, to write his memoirs and to do honour to his name by their inheritance of his qualities. It is difficult, however, to read those very memoirs without seeing that Garrison encountered in life some drawbacks which grew out of his own temperament, that he ceased in some cases to hold the warm friendships he had made, and lost the alliance of many of his early supporters; while Whittier during his whole life rarely lost a friend. That was true of him in life which Mr. Wendell has keenly said of him since his death, that "though a lifelong and earnest reformer, he is the least irritating of reformers to those who chance not to agree with him."[1] Garrison, again, had the experience, almost unique among reformers, of triumphing, as it were, in spite of himself and by ways which ran precisely counter to his own immediate methods and even predictions. A non-resistant, he saw his ends effected by war; a disunionist, he lived to join in the chorus of triumph over the reëstablishment of the American Union. Step by step, Whittier saw his own political opinions established; while Garrison lived to be content in seeing his specific counsels set aside and his aims accomplished by other methods than his own.

One of the most permanent qualities always to be relied upon in Whittier was his generosity in all matters of money, a thing peculiarly valuable in one who had learned in early life, by privation, to count his dollars very carefully. The following note to me, in regard to helping a young authoress, who had planned to go to her father, then in England, will well illustrate this. The note came undated, but was received in July, 1870.

"My dear H——, I quite agree with thee as regards our friend —— and wd. be glad to help her. I have reserved the sum of $50 for her when she needs it to go to England; but if she requires it now especially, I shall be happy to forward it at once, either to her or to thee, in which case thee can say that thee have rec'd that sum of me for her

[1] Wendell's "Literary History of America," p. 359.

benefit, which will leave her but $50 to repay [she being then $100 in debt].

"I got thy note as regards Boutwell [some political matter] yesterday, and shall write as thee suggest. I wish I could only straighten things out, in this snarl of a world. God help us! We can do but little, but that little shall not be withheld on our part.

"Always truly thy frd.

"JOHN G. WHITTIER.

"[P.S.] Advise me whether to send the money to her or to thee."

The very letter enclosing the money suggested also another object of interest, in a similar direction.

Some years later, on the marriage of the first young lady, this gift was duplicated, as seen by the following note — having the same combination, as before, of philanthropy and politics: —

"OAK KNOLL, DANVERS, 3d mo., 26, '78.

"MY DEAR HIGGINSON, — Thanks for thy letter. I have mislaid ——'s address. . . . Will thee drop me a postal to tell me? I will send her $50 as a wedding gift, as thee suggest. I am glad she is soon to escape from her desk drudgery.

"Thine always,

"J. G. W.

"If there is a change in the Cabinet I hope Evarts will go. He may be a lawyer — he seems to be nothing else. He has about as much magnetism as one of Dexter's wooden images. Washburn, late minister to France, would do well in the Cabinet, I think."

This was in early life, but after the sales of his poems became lucrative his income was large in proportion to his needs, — his personal expenditures increasing but slightly, — and he was, as his friends knew, most generous in giving. In this he was stimulated perhaps by the extraordinary example of his old friend, Mrs. Lydia Maria Child, whose letters he edited, and who used to deny herself many of the common comforts of advancing years in order that she might give to the works which interested her; yet Whittier was distinctly treading a similar path when he subscribed regularly and largely to General Armstrong's great enterprise for the instruction of the blacks and Indians at Hampton; and apart from this he was writing such letters as the following, all the time: —

"AMESBURY, 16th, 7th mo., 1870.

"DEAR HIGGINSON, — Enclosed find cheque for Fifty Dollars, $50. [This was for a person known to both of us.]

"I see by the *Transcript* that Phebe Cary lies very ill in Newport — dangerously, even. I do not know her address. I wish thee wd. find out, & call, & enquire about her, & leave her a message from me of love and sympathy, if she is in a condition to receive it. Poor girl! she gave herself to the care of her sister too unreservedly.

"Always & truly"
"thy fd
"JOHN G. WHITTIER."

The following is the account given of his kindness to a man, who described it anonymously in the *Literary World* for December 1877: —

"When I was a young man trying to get an education, I went about the country peddling sewing silk to help myself through college, and one Saturday night found me at Amesbury, a stranger and without a lodging-place. It happened that the first house at which I called was Whittier's, and he himself came to the door. On hearing my request, he said he was very sorry that he could not keep me, but it was Quarterly Meeting, and his house was full. He, however, took the trouble to show me to a neighbour's, where he left me; but that did not seem to wholly suit his ideas of hospitality, for in the course of the evening he made his appearance, saying that it had occurred to him that he could sleep on a lounge, and give up his own bed to me, — which it is, perhaps, needless to say, was not allowed. But this was not all. The next morning he came again, with the suggestion that I might perhaps like to attend meeting, inviting me to go with him; and he gave me a seat next to himself. The meeting lasted an hour, during which there was not a word spoken by any one. We all sat in silence that length of time, then all arose, shook hands, and dispersed; and I remember it as one of the best meetings I ever attended."[1]

No one came nearer to Whittier in all good deeds or in private intimacy than the late Mrs. Mary B. Claflin, well known in Boston and Washington, in both of which cities she exercised profuse hospitality, during the public life of her husband, the Hon. William Claflin. No book yields such a store of private anecdotes about Whittier as her little work, "Personal Recollections of John G. Whittier." Mrs. Claflin quotes one adviser, who said "I would rather give a man or woman on the verge of a great moral lapse a marked copy of Whittier than any other book in our language." She goes on to describe a young and over-sensitive college girl, overcome with the strain of her new life, who went to the president, and said, "It is of no use, I cannot go on, my life is a failure; I must leave college and go home." The tactful president replied, "Go to the library and take Whittier's poems, sit down by your window and read 'The Grave by the Lake,' then come and I will talk with you." The young girl came back in an hour with a changed

[1] Kennedy's "Whittier," pp. 167–68.

countenance. She said, "I will overcome the obstacles, I will go on with my college course. I believe, after reading Whittier, that life is worth the effort."

Mrs. Claflin adds another instance of a woman in prison, utterly wild with rage and excitement, who was wholly quieted by being persuaded to sit down and read Whittier's poem on "The Eternal Goodness."

These were Whittier's relations with those poorer or humbler than himself. He never visited princes, and so was not tested much in that direction, but I remember an occasion when an emperor once visited him. While Dom Pedro II., formerly emperor of Brazil, was in the United States in 1876, I had the pleasure of meeting him at George Bancroft's house in Newport, R.I., and remember well the desire that he expressed to see Whittier, and the comparative indifference with which he received our conversation on all other subjects. He had, it seems, translated Whittier's "Cry of a Lost Soul" into Portuguese. When, on June 14, they met at the Radical Club, at Rev. J. T. Sargent's, on Chestnut Street, the interview was thus described in Mrs. Sargent's record of the club: —

"When the emperor arrived, the other guests had already assembled. Sending up his card, his Majesty followed it with the quickness of an enthusiastic schoolboy; and his first question, after somewhat hastily paying his greetings, was for Mr. Whittier. The poet stepped forward to meet his imperial admirer, who would fain have caught him in his arms and embraced him warmly, with all the enthusiasm of the Latin race. The diffident Friend seemed somewhat abashed at so demonstrative a greeting, but with a cordial grasp of the hand drew Dom Pedro to the sofa, where the two chatted easily and with the familiarity of old friends.

"The rest of the company allowed them to enjoy their *tête-à-tête* for some half-hour, when they ventured to interrupt it, and the emperor joined very heartily in a general conversation.

"As the emperor was driving away, he was seen standing erect in his open barouche, and 'waving his hat, with a seeming hurrah, at the house which held his venerable friend.'"[1]

Mrs. Claflin tells us that Whittier, when her guest in his later life, received many letters — sometimes fifty — by the morning's mail, and describes one occasion where he lingered over a letter with a look of deep sympathy, and added "Such letters greatly humiliate me." It came from a lonely woman on a remote farm among the hills of New Hampshire, who aimed to tell him what his poems had done for her, and said: —

"In my darkest moments I have found light and comfort in your poems, which I always keep by my side, and as I never expect to have the privilege of looking into your face, I feel that I must tell you, before I leave this world, what you have been through your writings to one, and I have no doubt to many, a longing heart and homesick soul. I have never been in a place so dark and hopeless that I could not find light and comfort and hope in your poems, and when I go into my small room and close the door upon the worries and perplexing cares that constantly beset me, and sit down by my window that looks out over the hills which have been my only companions, I never fail to find in the volume which is always by my side some word of peace and comfort to my longing heart."

[1] Mrs. Sargent's "Sketches and Reminiscences of the Radical Club," pp. 301–02.

It was such communications as these which completed the influence of temperament, and made him appear to the world even more shy than he was. He used to say to Mrs. Claflin: —

"What does thee think women make such silly speeches to me for? It makes me feel like a fool. A woman said to me yesterday, 'Mr. Whittier, your smile is a benediction.' As I was walking across the floor at the Radical Club, a woman stopped me in the middle of the parlour among all the folks, and said, 'I've long wished to see you, Mr. Whittier, to ask what you thought of the subjective and the objective.' Why, I thought the woman was crazy, and I said, 'I don't know anything about either of 'em.'"

A young friend asked him one day if Mr. Fields's story were true about the woman who made her way to his library under pretence of conversing with him upon literary topics. "Mr. Fields said her conversation became very personal and tender, and you remarked, 'I do not understand thee, I do not understand thee; thee had better leave the room.' Was that really true, Mr. Whittier?" asked the young girl. With a very funny twinkle in his eye, he replied, "Does thee think, Mary, I could treat a lady in so ungentlemanly a manner as that?" That was the only response Mary could elicit.

Shy and self-withdrawing in conversation although Whittier might be, he was never caught at a disadvantage and was always ready with some pithy reply. If he had any one firm rule, it was to avoid making a speech, and yet when, being called on unexpectedly to speak at a private service on the death of Charles Sumner, he rose and told off-hand a story of a Scotch colonel, who, being interred with military honours, had an unfriendly regiment detailed to fire a salute over his grave, seeing which, an onlooker said, "If the colonel could have known this, he would not have died." — "So I feel," said Mr. Whittier. "If my friend Sumner could have known that I should have been asked to speak at his memorial service, he would not have died." And he resumed his seat. When, after the meeting, a friend spoke to him of the breathless silence which pervaded the audience, that they might catch every word, the poet quickly replied, "Don't thee think they would have listened just as attentively if Balaam's animal had spoken?"

The element of humour, which early showed itself in Whittier, was undoubtedly one influence which counteracted whatever element of narrowness was to be derived from his Quaker training. One sees how a fine mind may be limited in influence through the want of humour when considering such a case as that of the Rev. Dr. William Ellery Channing, for instance, whose writings, otherwise powerful, have gradually diminished in influence through such a deficiency. Possibly even Tufts and Burroughs may have been in some degree useful in their post-mortem career, by helping to cultivate this trait in the young poet. That he read Sterne and Swift with enjoyment, we know.

There is little evidence, however, that his early writings showed any trace of this gift. The dozen poems which he had written at eighteen, and the ninety-six printed within two years (1827–28) in the Haverhill *Gazette* alone, were apparently quite serious and sometimes solemn. "Exile," "Benevolence," "Ocean," "The Deity," "The Sicilian Vespers," "The Earthquake," "The Missionary," "Judith and Holofernes," these were the themes which, with much rhetoric and personification, were handled by the minstrel in his teens.

"Diffuse thy charms, Benevolence!"

was the cry, or more elaborately: —

"Hail, heavenly gift within the human breast!
Germ of unnumber'd virtues!"

This was the prevailing tone which had previously reached its climax in that humbler poet in England, whose appeal began with: —

"Inoculation! heavenly maid."

Coleridge and the rest of his circle went through this period of impassioned declamation, and Whittier could not hope to escape it.

At the dinners of the Atlantic Club, during the first few years of the magazine, I can testify that Whittier appeared as he always did, simple, manly, and unbecomingly shy, yet reticent and quiet. If he was overshadowed in talk by Holmes at one end and by Lowell at the other, he was in the position of every one else, notably Longfellow; but he had plenty of humour and critical keenness and there was no one whose summing up of the affairs afterward was better worth hearing. On the noted occasion, — the parting dinner given to Dr. and Mrs. Stowe, — the only one where wine was excluded save under disguise, I remember Whittier's glances of subdued amusement while Lowell at the end of the table was urging upon Mrs. Stowe the great superiority of "Tom Jones" to all other novels, and Holmes at the other end was demonstrating to the Rev. Dr. Stowe that all swearing really began in the too familiar use of holy words in the pulpit. His unmoved demeanour, as of a delegate sent from the Society of Friends to represent the gospel of silence among the most vivacious talkers, recalled Hazlitt's description of the supper parties at Charles Lamb's — parties which included Mrs. Reynolds, "who being of a quiet turn, loved to hear a noisy debate."[1]

[1] Hazlitt's essay, "On the Conversation of Authors."

CHAPTER IX

WHITTIER AT HOME

One of Whittier's biographers, Mr. William Sloane Kennedy, who has also been in a manner a biographer of Whitman, rather surprises the reader by an unexpected admission in comparing the two. He says of Whittier, "He is democratic, not so powerfully and broadly as Whitman, but more unaffectedly and sincerely." It is a concession of some value, the critic having been one of Whitman's warmest admirers and most generous advocates, and it seems to me to touch the truth very well. Certainly no one could see Whittier in contact with his fellow-citizens of a country village, without being struck by the genuineness and healthiness, so to speak, of the relations between them. If I may repeat my own words used elsewhere, I should say that there was something most satisfactory in the position of the poet among the village people. He was their pride and their joy, yet he lived as simply as any one, was careful and abstemious, reticent rather than exuberant in manner, and met them wholly on matter-of-fact ground. He could sit on a barrel and discuss the affairs of the day with the people who came to the "store," but he did not read them his verses. I was once expressing regrets for his ill health, in talking with one of the leading citizens of Amesbury, and found that my companion could not agree with me;

he thought that Whittier's ill health had helped him in the end, for it had "kept him from engaging in business," and had led him to writing poetry, which had given him reputation outside of the town. That poetry was anything but a second choice, perhaps a necessary evil, did not seem to have occurred to my informant. Had he himself lost his health and been unable to sell groceries, who knows but he too might have taken up with the Muses? It suggested the Edinburgh citizen who thought that Sir Walter Scott might have been "sic a respectable mon" had he stuck to his original trade of law advocate.

I will borrow from what I have elsewhere written a picture of the Whittier household as I saw it, more than fifty years ago, when residing at Newburyport in his neighbourhood.

"It was but a short walk or drive of a few miles from my residence to his home; or, better still, it implied a sail or row up the beautiful river, passing beneath the suspension bridge at Deer Island, to where the woods called 'The Laurels' spread themselves on one side, and the twin villages of Salisbury and Amesbury on the other. . . .

"To me, who sought Whittier for his poetry as well as his politics, nothing could have been more delightful than his plain abode with its exquisite Quaker neatness. His placid mother, rejoicing in her two gifted children, presided with few words at the hospitable board, whose tablecloth and napkins rivalled her soul in whiteness; and with her was the brilliant 'Lizzie,' so absolutely the reverse, or complement, of her brother that they seemed between them to make one soul. She was as plain in feature as he was handsome, except that she had a pair of great, luminous dark eyes, always flashing with fun or soft with emotion, and often changing with lightning rapidity from the one expression to the other; her nose was large and aquiline, while his was almost Grecian; and she had odd motions of the head, so that her glances seemed shot at you, like sudden javelins, from each side of a prominent network. Her complexion was sallow, not rich brunette like his; and whereas he spoke seldom and with difficulty, her gay raillery was unceasing, and was enjoyed by him as much as by anybody, so that he really appeared to have transferred to her the expression of his own opinions. . . . The lively utterances thus came with double force upon the auditor, and he could not fail to go out strengthened and stimulated. Sometimes the Whittiers had guests; and 'Lizzie' delighted to tell how their mother was once met at the door by two plump maidens, who announced that they had come from Ohio mainly to see her son. She explained that he was in Boston. No matter; they would come in and await his return. But he might be away a week. No matter; they would willingly wait that time for such a pleasure. So in they came. They proved to be Alice and Phœbe Cary, whose earlier poems, which had already preceded them, were filled with dirges and despair; but they were the merriest of housemates, and as the poet luckily returned next day, they stayed as long as they pleased, and were welcome."

It is hardly fair, however, to give this last incident without giving the letter by which the unwary bachelor poet brought this visit upon his household. He had actually invited these frank young ladies by the following letter, not put in print for many years after, and addressed to that general friend — and occasional enemy — of all literary people, Rufus Wilmot Griswold, of New York: —

"AMESBURY, 21st JUNE, 1850.

"MY DEAR FR. GRISWOLD: — I learn from my friend F. W. Kellogg that Alice and Phœbe Cary, of Ohio, are on their way to the East, and would be glad to see them at my place if they come to Boston. Presuming that thou wilt see them in N.Y. I have taken the liberty to invite them, through thee, to call on me. I have been quite ill this spring and my sister also is an invalid, and we see little company, but I should feel sorry to have the 'sweet singers' of the West so near and not see them.

"Dost ever come to Boston? I should be very glad to see thee at Amesbury. I have a pleasant and grateful recollection of our acquaintance in N.Y. and Boston. I shall be obliged to thee if thou wilt kindly remember me to Tuckerman. I like his last book exceedingly, and shall notice it soon in the *Era*.

"Thine cordially,

"JOHN G. WHITTIER."[1]

A lady who had been long a neighbour once described Whittier's parlour fire: —

"That fire was a perpetual source of pleasure and annoyance to us all. It was an old-fashioned Franklin stove, that smoked on the slightest provocation, and scattered the ashes over the hearth. At the same time it had a habit of throwing out the most charming gleams and shadows, especially if driftwood was being burned. Mr. Whittier was very jealous of any one else tending or poking the fire. Often I have unconsciously taken the tongs to touch up a brand, when his hand would stay mine, and he would say, 'Thee must not touch that, it is just right,' and perhaps the next minute he would have the tongs and do just what I had attempted. I have frequently gone in at twilight and found him lying on the lounge, watching the flitting shadows, and repeating aloud from some favourite author, generally Scott or Burns. His mood and conversation at such times were particularly delightful. The beautiful poem, 'Burning Driftwood' was doubtless inspired by such experiences."[2]

One of the very best delineations of Whittier by one of those who approached him on the public or semi-public side is that written by the Hon. Robert S. Rantoul of Salem, Mass.: —

[1] Letters of R. W. Griswold, pp. 266–67. [2] Pickard, II. 745.

"Mr. Whittier was self-contained. In the company of persons whom he did not care for — who could not draw him out — his mind seemed to furnish him with almost nothing to say. He had no small talk. Where there was nothing in common he could be as remote and silent as a mountain peak. . . . For himself, he was transparent in his expressions and he sought the communion of those only who met him on his own ground. Insincerity was incivility. . . .

"He could no more face a mixed company than he could face an audience. It was the lack of touch — of correlation — that seemed to disturb him. Miss Bremer said of him that he could cheerfully confront martyrdom, but shrank from the ordinary requirements of social intercourse. . . .

"Later, in 1882, when I was a member of the Republican State Central Committee, I was designated to conduct Mr. Whittier from his rooms in Boston on the morning of the Music Hall convention which put Robinson forward for the defeat of Butler, and I was specially charged to place him in a conspicuous seat near the front of the platform, that all Massachusetts might see that he was with us. By dint of much entreaty and persuasion I finally prevailed. No man was better entitled to a high seat in the party sanhedrim at that time, nor more worthy to be held up as the high priest of Massachusetts Republicanism. But the proceedings were scarcely opened when I found his chair was vacant. He had stolen away to a hiding-place beside the great organ, where he could see and hear without being discovered, and the convention from that time on, so far as its visual faculties availed, was without its poet."

We have, through Mrs. Claflin, also Whittier's own reports as to his personal conversations with fellow-authors. For instance, as he was driving one day with Emerson, the latter pointed out a small, unpainted house by the roadside, and said: —

"'There lives an old Calvinist in that house, and she says she prays for me every day. I am glad she does. I pray for myself.' 'Does thee?' said Whittier. 'What does thee pray for, friend Emerson?'

"'Well,' replied Emerson, 'when I first open my eyes upon the morning meadows, and look out upon the beautiful world, I thank God that I am alive, and that I live so near Boston.'"

In one of their conversations, Mr. Emerson remarked that the world had not yet seen the highest development of manhood.

"'Does thee think so?' said Whittier. 'I suppose thee would admit that Jesus Christ is the highest development our world has seen?'

"'Yes, yes, but not the highest it will see.'

"'Does thee think the world has yet reached the ideals the Christ has set for mankind?'

"'No, no,' said Emerson: 'I think not.'

"'Then is it not the part of wisdom to be content with what has been given us, till we have lived up to that ideal? And when we need something higher, Infinite Wisdom will supply our needs.'"

Amesbury, like Concord, had its individual oddities; and the two poets liked to compare notes upon them. Whittier had a neighbour whose original remarks he loved to repeat, and Emerson once said, "That man ought to read Plato," and offered him a volume through Whittier. It was kept for a while and then returned with the remark, "There are some good things in that book. I find that this Mr. Plato has a good many of my ideas."

Whittier gave to Mrs. Claflin, also, this account of his only advance toward personal intercourse with Hawthorne: —

"He said, 'Thee knows I am not skilled in visits and small talk, but I wanted to make a friendly call on Hawthorne, and one morning — it chanced to be an ill-fated morning for this purpose — I sallied forth, and on reaching the house was ushered into a lugubrious-looking room where Hawthorne met me, evidently in a lugubrious state of mind.

"'In rather a sepulchral tone of voice he bade me good-morning, and asked me to be seated opposite him, and we looked at each other and remarked upon the weather; then came an appalling silence and the cold chills crept down my back, and after a moment or two I got up and said, "I think I will take a short walk." I took my walk and returned to bid him good morning much to my relief, and I have no doubt to his.'"

With Mrs. Stowe he would sit till the small hours of the morning, and till the lights burned blue, to talk about psychical mysteries, and relate stories of ghosts and spirit rappings and manifestations. They "wooed the courteous ghosts" together; but he said, "Much as I have wooed them, they never appear to me. Mrs. Stowe is more fortunate — the spirits sometimes come at her bidding, but never at mine — and what wonder? It would be a foolish spirit that did not prefer her company to that of an old man like me." They would repeat, says Mrs. Claflin, the most marvellous stories of ghostly improbabilities, apparently for the time being believing every word. With Mrs. Elizabeth Stuart Phelps Ward, who had written on the possible employments of another life, he would discuss that theme with a relish, but would add, "Elizabeth, thee would not be happy in heaven unless thee could go missionary to the other place, now and then."

Quakers, if genuine, usually have rather a predilection for fighters. Garibaldi was one of Whittier's heroes, so was General Gordon, so was young Colonel Shaw; and so was John Bright, who fought with words only. Whittier wrote at his death to Mrs. Fields:—

"Spring is here to-day, warm, birdful. . . . It seems strange that I am alive to welcome her when so many have passed away with the winter, and among them that stalwartest of Englishmen, John Bright, sleeping now in the daisied grounds of Rochdale, never more to move the world with his surpassing eloquence. How I regret that I have never seen him! We had much in common in our religious faith, our hatred of war and oppression. His great genius seemed to me to be always held firmly in hand by a sense of duty, and by the practical common sense of a shrewd man of business. He fought through life like an old knight-errant, but without enthusiasm. He had no personal ideals. I remember once how he remonstrated with me for my admiration for General Gordon. He looked upon that wonderful personality as a wild fighter, a rash adventurer, doing evil that good might come. He could not see him as I saw him, giving his life for humanity, alone and unfriended, in that dreadful Soudan. He did not like the idea of fighting Satan with Satan's weapons. Lord Salisbury said truly that John Bright was the greatest orator England had produced, and his eloquence was only called out by what he regarded as the voice of God in his soul."[1]

It is an interesting fact that one of the best pictures ever drawn of Whittier in his home life is that drawn by Hayne, the Southern poet, who once visited him.

"So 'neath the Quaker poet's tranquil roof,
From all deep discords of the world aloof,
I sit once more and measured converse hold,
With him whose nobler thoughts are rhythmic gold;
See his deep brows half-puckered in a knot,
O'er some hard problem of our mortal lot,
Or a dream soft as May winds of the south,
Waft a girl's sweetness 'round his firm, set mouth.

[1] Mrs. Fields's "Whittier," pp. 50–51.

"Or, should he deem wrong threats the public weal,
Lo, the whole man seems girt with flashing steel;
His glance a sword-thrust and his words of ire,
Like thunder tones from some old prophet's lyre.
Or by the hearthstone, when the day is done,
Mark swiftly lanced a sudden shaft of fun;
The short quick laugh, the smartly smitten knees,
Are all sure tokens of a mind at ease.

"God's innocent pensioners in the woodland dim,
The fields, the pastures, know and trust in him,
And in their love, his lonely heart is blest,
Our pure hale-minded Cowper of the West."

CHAPTER X

THE RELIGIOUS SIDE

WHITTIER, as has already been seen, was born and brought up in the Society of Friends, of which he always remained a faithful member. In trying to solve the problem, how far he felt himself strictly bound by the usages of his Society, the following anecdote, as told by Mr. Pickard, is suggestive. On the night before the burning of Pennsylvania Hall in 1838, in Philadelphia, as an antislavery headquarters, there occurred the marriage of Angelina Grimké to Theodore D. Weld, both being afterwards prominent antislavery reformers. Miss Grimké was a South Carolina Quakeress, who had liberated her own slaves, and was thenceforward known far and wide as an antislavery lecturer, but her proposed husband was not a Quaker. At the time of her wedding, Whittier, who then edited the *Freeman*, was invited to attend; but as she was marrying "out of society," he did not think it fitting that he should be present at the ceremony. He nevertheless reconciled it with his conscience to escort a young lady to the door, and to call on the wedded pair, next day, with a congratulatory poem.[1] This fairly indicates the hold his early religious training had upon him, when the question was one of outward observances alone.

In reading, not merely Whittier's meditative and spiritual poems, but the very texts and preludes which

[1] Pickard's "Whittier," I. 235.

are prefixed to them, one feels the immense advantage enjoyed by those brought up in the Society of Friends, as to a simpler and therefore more sacred use of the Hebrew and Christian scriptures, than was possible to those trained in the more rigorous and severe methods which prevailed so largely in his youth among the evangelical sects. His citations of passages are superb in their discrimination; the words of Ezekiel and Esdras seem greater and profounder than those of his verses that follow; and yet this is no truer of them than of the prefatory prelude taken from St. Augustine, or George Fox, or the Hymns of the Brahmo-Somaj. This is as it should be; that the poet's gift should show itself even in the texts of his sermons; yet no one who had not learned to reverence the Inward Light as the Society of Friends did, could follow it, even to the selection of good texts.

He was a firm but liberal Quaker, would carry out to the utmost the original standard, regarded as useless the division between Orthodox and Hicksite, and predicted that tendency to reunion which now shows itself. He was, on the other hand, never quite reconciled to the new departures in manner and observance which have marked the last twenty years. When asked as to Quaker variations from the ordinary grammar, he replied, according to Mrs. Claflin: —

"'It has been the manner of speech of my people for two hundred years; it was my mother's language, and it is good enough for me; I shall not change my grammar.' So in coming from a Quaker meeting one day in a state of great indignation, he said, 'Our folks have got to talking t' much; they even want a glass of water on the table, and some of them want singing in the meetings. I tell them if they want singing, they have got to get the world's folks to do it for them, for two hundred years of silence have taken all the sing out of our people."

Yet the manner in which historic extremes have so often met was never more strangely exhibited than in a fact in early Quaker tradition revealed by Whittier to Mrs. Fields. In speaking of Rossetti and his extraordinary mediæval ballad of "Sister Helen," Whittier confessed himself strongly attracted to it, because he could remember seeing his mother, "who was as good a woman as ever breathed," with his aunt, performing the strange act on which the ballad turns, and melting a waxen figure of a clergyman of their time, that his soul might go to its doom in hell. "The solemnity of the affair made a deep impression on his mind, as a child, for the death of the clergyman in question was confidently expected. His 'heresies' had led him to experience this cabalistic treatment."[1] The aim of the mystic ceremony was to destroy the soul of the passing invalid, and it seems almost incredible that any sight or memory of human suffering should have called forth such a spirit of revenge in those seemingly gentle women. No one who has ever read the tragic close of Rossetti's song can ever forget it.

"'See, see, the wax has dropped from its place,
Sister Helen,
And the waves are winning up apace!'
'Yet here they burn but for a space,
Little brother!'
(O Mother, Mary, Mother,
Here for a space, between Hell and Heaven!)

[1] Mrs. Fields's "Whittier," p. 52.

"'Ah! what white thing at the door has cross'd,
Sister Helen?
Ah! what is this that sighs in the frost?'
'A soul that's lost as mine is lost,
Little brother!'
(*O Mother, Mary, Mother,*
Lost, lost, all lost, between Hell and Heaven.)"

It is evident, however, that Whittier had in early life some vague vision of an intellectual movement which should enlarge the atmosphere of the Society of Friends, not, as has since been done, in the methodistical or camp-meeting direction — for that he disapproved — but in the direction of a higher thought and life. This letter, hitherto unpublished, from one of the most gifted and cultivated associates in his Quaker years, reveals to us indirectly this mood of his, and is well worth printing because it mirrors his own mood. It may be well to add that the writer left the Society, not many years after, and apparently retained but little affection for it, going so far as to say once to me, "Quakerism makes splendid women, and very poor, mean, miserable men;" from which general condemnation Whittier was exempted, although in later years their friendship apparently waned, and she seemed hardly to appreciate him at his great worth.

"I am delighted with thy idea, Greenleaf — and it is strange that thou shouldst have given form and substance to a vague desire that has often floated thro' my brain, of seeing something like a corner-stone laid for a Quaker temple of literature. And thou art the man to undertake it — to humour the 'anti-imaginative' spirit of thine own people, and at the same time, by thy *peculiar touches* of strength and beauty, to expand our inherent tendencies toward *mere* truth and soberness, into a stronger love, that will produce good works, of the self-forgetting *nobleness* of primitive Quakerism.

"The varieties in the natural characters of our forefathers, some of those thee mentioned, would be good ground for the *beautiful*. The depth and fervour and intensity of their love to God, which sent them forth, even while their human heart-strings were quivering and cracking with agony, to the dungeon and to death, in the cause of Truth, would befit the lofty and sublime.

"The agency and influence which their doctrines exerted in bursting the coil that the lumbering superstitions of the past had wrapped about the human mind at the time of their arising — though so much built upon *now* by their ease-loving followers, might be justly and strikingly brought into view; and this would be the part for the world — those amongst men, who consider Quakerism but another name for narrowmindedness and bigotry, and the doctrine of human rights, as understood and advocated by our noble pioneer, the far-seeing Penn, and others, but treason.

"The character of our women too, their beautiful faith, devotedness, and fortitude, which come, not of the sect, but by nature, would most fittingly adorn the annals of Quakerism. Thee would not approve the *monthly meeting* cant, or have anything of our ludicrous quaintness, wouldst thou? but rather lay the foundation for a pure and correct taste, than minister to one, [old] and vitiated.

"I have never seen the Wordsworth sonnets alluded to, but will look at them, to understand thy place.

"Thy idea only wants the setting of J. G. Whittier's poetry to make it the richest jewel on his crown of fame. But I would have thee lay it by, uncut and unpolished, till restored health and the quiet occupations of a *home life* will allow thee to work upon it without paying the price, which has been the penalty of too many of thy literary labours.

"Thee had a double motive, hadst thou not, in mentioning the subject? one, for its own interest, and the other to remind me that it is not good for us to dwell too much upon our own little petty grievances. Thanks for the hint;

nothing, in kindness and good feeling sent, comes amiss to me, whether it be unmerited praise, or deserved reproof.

"THY FRIEND.

"4th day morning."

We know from Whittier's own statement that while his parents governed by love rather than by fear, yet even he did not fail to encounter in childhood terrors on the supernatural side. Books brought them, if they had no other source, as we find revealed, for instance, in this reminiscence, forming a part of his "Supernaturalism in New England:" —

"How hardly effaced are the impressions of childhood! Even at this day, at the mention of the evil angel, an image rises before me like that with which I used especially to horrify myself in an old copy of 'Pilgrim's Progress.' Horned, hoofed, scaly, and fire-breathing, his caudal extremity twisted tight with rage, I remember him, illustrating the tremendous encounter of Christian in the valley where 'Apollyon straddled over the whole breadth of the way.' There was another print of the enemy which made no slight impression upon me. It was the frontispiece of an old, smoked, snuff-stained pamphlet, the property of an elderly lady, who had a fine collection of similar wonders, wherewith she was kind enough to edify her young visitors, containing a solemn account of the fate of a wicked dancing party in New Jersey, whose irreverent declaration, that they would have a fiddler if they had to send to the lower regions after him, called up the fiend himself, who forthwith commenced playing, while the company danced to the music incessantly, without the power to suspend their exercise, until their feet and legs were worn off to the knees! The rude wood-cut represented the demon fiddler and his agonised companions literally *stumping* it up and down in 'cotillons, jigs, strathspeys, and reels.' He would have answered very well to the description of the infernal piper in 'Tam O' Shanter.'"

The best impression of Whittier's relation with the Society of Friends will be found in two letters addressed by him, in later life, to the editor of the *Friends' Review* in Philadelphia, in reference to the changes then beginning, and maturing later, and destined to transform so greatly the whole society. Those who were acquainted with that body in its earlier state, and saw the steps by which it was, in the judgment of its reformers, modernised and invigorated, can well understand the point of view of Whittier, who certainly represented not merely its most elevated, but its most practical and progressive side. I remember well at Newport at the very time described by him (1870) to have seen incidents which almost burlesqued the ancient faith, as when a schoolgirl of fourteen sat eating candy busily during the exercises, and on hearing the stentorian voice of a Western revivalist to "Stand up for Jesus," put her candy down on the seat beside her, rose and bore her testimony, and then want back eagerly to her candy, once more; or when the ablest and most justly influential of the society, the late Edward Earle of Worcester, rose toward the end of the meeting and proposed that after the custom of their fathers they should take a few silent moments. He had scarcely sat down when one of the same New Lights rose behind him and struck up a rousing camp-meeting song, in which all silent thought vanished. It was under just such provocations as these that Whittier wrote, these were the charges against which Whittier protested; and, as will be seen, in the same just and moderate tone which usually marked his writings.

The following letters were addressed to the editor

of the *Friends' Review* in Philadelphia, in reference to certain changes of principle and practice in the Society then beginning to be observable, but which have since more than justified the writer's fears and solicitude.

"AMESBURY, 2nd mo., 1870.

"TO THE EDITOR OF THE *Review*.

"ESTEEMED FRIEND, — I have been hitherto a silent, I have not been an indifferent, spectator of the movements now going on in our religious Society. Perhaps from lack of faith, I have been quite too solicitous concerning them, and too much afraid that in grasping after new things we may let go of old things too precious to be lost. Hence I have been pleased to see from time to time in thy paper very timely and fitting articles upon a 'Hired Ministry' and 'Silent Worship.'

The present age is one of sensation and excitement, of extreme measures and opinions, of impatience of all slow results. The world about us moves with accelerated impulse, and we move with it: the rest we have enjoyed, whether true or false, is broken; the title-deeds of our opinions, the reason of our practices, are demanded. Our very right to exist as a distinct society is questioned. Our old literature — the precious journals and biographies of early and later Friends — is comparatively neglected for sensational and dogmatic publications. We hear complaints of a want of educated ministers; the utility of silent meetings is denied, and praying and preaching regarded as matters of will and option. There is a growing desire for experimenting upon the dogmas and expedients and practices of other sects. I speak only of admitted facts, and not for the purpose of censure or complaint. No one has less right than myself to indulge in heresy-hunting or impatience of minor differences of opinion. If my dear friends can bear with me, I shall not find it a hard task to bear with them.

"But for myself I prefer the old ways. With the broadest possible tolerance for all honest seekers after truth, I love the Society of Friends. My life has been nearly spent in labouring with those of other sects in behalf of the suffering and enslaved; and I have never felt like quarrelling with Orthodox or Unitarians, who were willing to pull with me, side by side, at the rope of Reform. A very large proportion of my dearest personal friends are outside of our communion; and I have learned with John Woolman to find 'no narrowness respecting sects and opinions.' But after a kindly and candid survey of them all, I turn to my own Society, thankful to the Divine Providence which placed me where I am; and with an unshaken faith in the one distinctive doctrine of Quakerism — the Light within — the immanence of the Divine Spirit in Christianity.

"I am not insensible of the need of spiritual renovation in our Society. I feel and confess my own deficiencies as an individual member. And I bear a willing testimony to the zeal and devotion of some dear friends, who, lamenting the low condition and worldliness too apparent among us, seek to awaken a stronger religious life by the partial adoption of the practices, forms, and creeds of more demonstrative sects. The great apparent activity of these sects seems to them to contrast very strongly with our quietness and reticence; and they do not always pause to inquire whether the result of this activity is a truer type of practical Christianity than is found in our select gatherings. I think I understand these brethren; to some extent I have sympathised with them. But it seems clear to me, that a remedy for the alleged evil lies not in going back to the 'beggarly elements' from which our worthy ancestors called the people of their generation; not in will-worship; not in setting the letter above the spirit; not in substituting type and symbol, and oriental figure and hyperbole for the simple truths they were intended to represent; not in schools of theology; not in much speaking and noise and vehemence, nor in vain attempts to make the 'plain language' of Quakerism utter the Shibboleth of man-made creeds: but in heeding more closely the Inward Guide and Teacher; in faith in Christ not merely in His historical manifestation of the Divine

Love to humanity, but in His living presence in the hearts open to receive Him; in love for Him manifested in denial of self, in charity and love to our neighbour; and in a deeper realisation of the truth of the apostle's declaration: 'Pure religion and undefiled before God and the Father is this, to visit the fatherless and widows in their affliction, and to keep himself unspotted from the world.'"

In a second letter he acknowledges many expressions of sympathy, and adds: —

"I believe that the world needs the Society of Friends as a testimony and a standard. I know that this is the opinion of some of the best and most thoughtful members of other Christian sects. I know that any serious departure from the original foundation of our Society would give pain to many who, outside of our communion, deeply realise the importance of our testimonies. They fail to read clearly the signs of the times who do not see that the hour is coming when, under the searching eye of philosophy and the terrible analysis of science, the letter and the outward evidence will not altogether avail us; when the surest dependence must be upon the Light of Christ within, disclosing the law and the prophets in our own souls, and confirming the truth of outward Scripture by inward experience; when smooth stones from the brook of present revelation shall prove mightier than the weapons of Saul; when the doctrine of the Holy Spirit, as proclaimed by George Fox and lived by John Woolman, shall be recognised as the only efficient solvent of doubts raised by an age of restless inquiry. In this belief my letter was written. I am sorry it did not fall to the lot of a more fitting hand; and can only hope that no consideration of lack of qualification on the part of its writer may lessen the value of whatever testimony to truth shall be found in it.

"Amesbury, 3d mo., 1870."[1]

By the testimony of all, Whittier's interpretation of "The Inward Light" included no vague recognition

[1] Whittier's "Prose Works," III. 305, 306, 309, 310, 313, 314.

of high impulse, but something definite, firm, and extending into the details of conduct. It ruled his action; and when he had, for instance, decided to take a certain railway train, no storm could keep him back. He used to cite the following instance, written out by Mrs. Claflin, of the trustworthiness of such guidance: —

"'I have an old friend,' he said, 'who followed the leadings of the Spirit and always made it a point to go to meeting on First-Day. On one First-Day morning, he made ready for meeting, and suddenly turning to his wife, said, "I am not going to meeting: I am going to take a walk." His wife inquired where he was going, and he replied, "I don't know; I am impelled to go, I know not where." With his walking stick he started and went out of the city for a mile or two, and came to a country-house that stood some distance from the road. The gate stood open, and a narrow lane, into which he turned, led up to the house where something unusual seemed to be going on. There were several vehicles standing around the yard, and groups of people were gathered here and there. When he reached the house, he found there was a funeral, and he entered with the neighbours, who were there to attend the service. He listened to the funeral address and to the prayer. It was the body of a young woman lying in the casket before him, and he arose and said, "I have been led by the Spirit to this house; I know nothing of the circumstances connected with the death of this person; but I am impelled by the Spirit to say that she has been accused of something of which she is not guilty, and the false accusation has hastened her death."

"'The friend sat down, and a murmur of surprise went through the room. The minister arose and said, "Are you a God or what *are* you?" The friend replied, "I am only a poor sinful man, but I was led by the Inner Light to come to this house, and to say what I have said, and I would ask the person in this room who knows that the young woman, now beyond the power of speech, was not guilty of what she was accused, to vindicate her in this presence." After a fearful pause, a woman stood up and said, "I am the person," and while weeping hysterically, she confessed that she had wilfully slandered the dead girl. The friend departed on his homeward way. Such,' said Mr. Whittier, 'was the leading of the Inner Light.'"[1]

There is clearly but a narrow step between these marvels and the alleged facts of spiritualism about which his placid old mother was so interested that she never failed, whenever I called there, to look up from her knitting after a while and say, "Friend Higginson, hast thee heard anything lately about these spiritual communications of which I hear?" the place where I then resided having been the scene of some reported marvels. Whittier also approached them in a guarded way, but without any very positive interest. He wrote once to Mrs. Fields, in regard to a poem she had sent him: —

"The poem is solemn and tender; it is as if a wind from the Unseen World blew over it, in which the voice of sorrow is sweeter than that of gladness — a holy fear mingled with a holier hope. For myself, my hope is always associated with dread, like the glowing of a star through mist. I feel, indeed, that Love is victorious, that there is no dark it cannot light, no depth it cannot reach; but I imagine that, between the Seen and the Unseen, there is a sort of neutral ground, a land of shadow and mystery, of strange voices and undistinguished forms. There are some, as Charles Lamb says, 'who stalk into futurity on stilts,' without awe or self-distrust."[2]

Judge Cate also writes me in regard to Whittier's supposed interest in "spiritual manifestations," as follows: —

[1] Claflin's "Recollections," p. 31.

[2] Mrs. Fields's "Whittier," p. 91.

"In regard to spiritualism. I think it can be truly said that Mr. Whittier was not a believer in spiritualism, but he acknowledged that there was something about it which he could not explain and did not understand. He frequently related the following incident. When in Boston, at the hotel one evening he met an old friend who was interested in spiritualism, and he asked Mr. Whittier to visit a medium with him; not being well that evening he declined, but late in the evening his friend returned. Mr. Whittier asked whom he saw. 'Well,' he replied, 'I saw Henry Wilson.' 'Did you? What did Henry have to say?' 'He spoke of you in very complimentary terms.' 'What did he say about me?' 'He said if he were to live his life over again he would pattern more after you, because he thought you had made less mistakes in your political life than any one he had known.' And Mr. Whittier said that this statement agreed substantially with a statement which Mr. Wilson made a short time before his death. He always spoke of spiritualism as something to be explained, while in his religious life he was indefinite about embracing any particular tenet outside of the Friends."[1]

Mrs. Fields describes him at that summer watering-place, the Isles of Shoals, as being once moved, which he rarely was, to volunteer his thoughts on spiritual subjects: —

"I remember one season in particular, when the idle talk of idle people had been drifting in and out during the day, while he sat patiently on in the corner of the pretty room. Mrs. Thaxter was steadily at work at her table, yet always hospitable, losing sight of no cloud or shadow or sudden gleam of glory in the landscape, and pointing the talk often with keen wit. Nevertheless, the idleness of it all palled upon him. It was Sunday, too, and he longed for something which would move us to 'higher levels.' Suddenly, as if the idea had struck him like an inspiration, he rose, and taking a volume of Emerson from the little library, he

[1] Ms. letter, Aug. 26, 1902.

opened to one of the discourses, and handing it to Celia Thaxter, said: —

"'Read that aloud, will thee? I think we should all like to hear it.'

"After she had ended he took up the thread of the discourse, and talked long and earnestly upon the beauty and necessity of worship — a necessity consequent upon the nature of man, upon his own weakness, and his consciousness of the Divine Spirit within him. His whole heart was stirred, and he poured himself out toward us as if he longed, like the prophet of old, to breathe a new life into us. I could see that he reproached himself for not having spoken out in this way before, but his enfranchised spirit took only a stronger flight for the delay.

"I have never heard of Whittier's speaking in the meeting-house, although he was doubtless often 'moved' to do so, but to us who had heard him on that day he became more than ever a light unto our feet. It was not an easy thing to do to stem the accustomed current of life in this way, and it is a deed only possible to those who, in the Bible phrase, 'walk with God.'

"Such an unusual effort was not without its consequences. It was followed by a severe headache, and he was hardly seen abroad again during his stay."[1]

The following letter to his friend Charlotte Fiske Bates — afterward Madame Roger — conveys most fully his point of view as to immortality.

"To Charlotte Fiske Bates.

"1879.

"I suppose nine out of ten of really thoughtful people, were they to express their real feeling, would speak much as thee do, of the mingled 'dread and longing' with which they look forward to the inevitable surrender of life. Of course, temperament and present surroundings have much influence with us. There are some self-satisfied souls who, as Charles Lamb says, 'can stalk into futurity on stilts'; but there are

[1] Mrs. Fields's "Whittier," pp. 75–77.

more Fearings and Despondencys than Greathearts in view of the 'loss of all we know.' I have heard Garrison talk much of his faith in spiritualism. He had no doubts whatever, and he was very happy. Death was to him but the passing from one room to another and higher one. But his *facts* did not convince me. I am slow to believe new things, and in a matter of such tremendous interest, I want 'assurance doubly sure.' I wonder whether, if I could see a real ghost, I should believe my own senses. I do sometimes feel very near to dear ones who have left me — perhaps they are with me then. I am sure they would be, if it were possible. Of one thing I feel sure: that something outside of myself speaks to me, and holds me to duty; warns, reproves, and approves. It is good, for it requires me to be good; it is wise, for it knows the thoughts and intents of the heart. It is to me a revelation of God, and of His character and attributes; the one important *fact*, before which all others seem insignificant. I have seen little or nothing of what is called Spiritualism. . . .

"I have no longer youth and strength, and I have not much to hope for, as far as this life is concerned; but I enjoy life. 'It is a pleasant thing to behold the sun.' I love Nature in her varied aspects; and, as I grow older, I find much to love in my fellow creatures, and also more to pity. I have the instinct of immortality, but the conditions of that life are unknown. I cannot conceive what my own identity and that of dear ones gone before me will be. And then the unescapable sense of sin in thought and deed, and doubtless some misconception of the character of God, makes the boldest of us cowards. Does thee remember the epitaph-prayer of Martin Elginbrod?

"'Here lie I, Martin Elginbrod;
Have pity on my soul, Lord God,
As I wad do were I Lord God
An' ye were Martin Elginbrod.'

"I think there is a volume of comfort in that verse. We Christians seem less brave and tranquil, in view of death, than the old Stoic sages. Witness Marcus Antoninus. I wonder if the creed of Christendom is really the 'glad tidings of great joy to all people' which the angels sang of. For myself, I believe in God as Justice, Goodness, Tenderness — in one word, Love; and yet, my trust in Him is not strong enough to overcome the natural shrinking from the law of death. Even our Master prayed that that cup might pass from Him, 'if it were possible.'"[1]

He said once to Mrs. Claflin: —

"The little circumstance of death will make no difference with me: I shall have the same friends in that other world that I have here; the same loves and aspirations and occupations. If it were not so, I should not be myself, and surely, I shall not lose my identity. God's love is so infinitely greater than mine that I cannot fear for His children, and when I long to help some poor, suffering, erring fellow-creature, I am consoled with the thought that His great heart of love is more moved than mine can be, and so I rest in peace."[2]

This is in harmony with his lines in "The Eternal Goodness" — lines which are oftener quoted, perhaps, than anything he wrote.

"I know not where His islands lift
 Their fronded palms in air;
I only know I cannot drift
 Beyond His love and care."

This is only a versification of what he wrote in a letter, in his eightieth year. "The great question of the Future Life is almost ever with me. I cannot answer it, but I can *trust*."

It is perhaps the natural outcome of a somewhat shy and self-withdrawn life that Whittier should have described himself in verse more frankly than any other of the poets, thus concentrating into one utterance of words what others, Holmes for instance, might

[1] Pickard's "Whittier," II. 651–53. [2] Claflin, p. 22.

distribute over a hundred scattered talks. He has never done this, however, with undue self-consciousness, but simply, frankly, and with an acute and delicate comprehension of his own traits. His poem "My Namesake," written in 1853, is the most elaborate of these delineations, and was addressed to his young namesake, Francis Greenleaf Allinson, of Burlington, N.J. These are some of the many verses: —

"And thou, dear child, in riper days
When asked the reason of thy name,
Shalt answer; 'One 'twere vain to praise
Or censure bore the same.

"'Some blamed him, some believed him good,
The truth lay doubtless 'twixt the two;
He reconciled as best he could
Old faith and fancies new.

"'In him the grave and playful mixed,
And wisdom held with folly truce,
And Nature compromised betwixt
Good fellow and recluse.

"'He loved his friends, forgave his foes;
And, if his words were harsh at times,
He spared his fellow-men, — his blows
Fell only on their crimes.

"'He loved the good and wise, but found
His human heart to all akin
Who met him on the common ground
Of suffering and of sin.

"'Whate'er his neighbours might endure
Of pain or grief his own became;
For all the ills he could not cure
He held himself to blame.

* * * * * *

"'But still his heart was full of awe
And reverence for all sacred things;
And, brooding over form and law,
He saw the Spirit's wings!

"'Life's mystery wrapt him like a cloud;
He heard far voices mock his own,
The sweep of wings unseen, the loud,
Long roll of waves unknown.'"

Literature has few finer meditative poems than that written in 1871, and bearing the name "My Birthday." Not a verse of this can well be spared for those who would be in intimate contact with the poet's soul.

"MY BIRTHDAY

"Beneath the moonlight and the snow
Lies dead my latest year;
The winter winds are wailing low,
It dirges in my ear.

"I grieve not with the moaning wind
As if a loss befell;
Before me, even as behind,
God is, and all is well!

"His light shines on me from above,
His low voice speaks within, —
The patience of immortal love
Outwearying mortal sin.

"Not mindless of the growing years
Of care and loss and pain,
My eyes are wet with thankful tears
For blessings which remain.

"If dim the gold of life has grown,
I will not count it dross,
Nor turn from treasures still my own
To sigh for lack and loss.

"The years no charm from Nature take ;
As sweet her voices call,
As beautiful her mornings break,
As fair her evenings fall.

"Love watches o'er my quiet ways,
Kind voices speak my name,
And lips that find it hard to praise
Are slow, at least, to blame.

"How softly ebb the tides of will!
How fields, once lost or won,
Now lie behind me green and still
Beneath a level sun !

"How hushed the hiss of party hate,
The clamour of the throng !
How old, harsh voices of debate
Flow into rhythmic song !

"Methinks the spirit's temper grows
Too soft in this still air ;
Somewhat the restful heart foregoes
Of needed watch and prayer.

"The bark by tempest vainly tossed
May founder in the calm,
And he who braved the polar frost
Faint by the isles of balm.

"Better than self-indulgent years
The outflung heart of youth,
Than pleasant songs in idle ears
The tumult of the truth.

"Rest for the weary hands is good,
And love for hearts that pine,
But let the manly habitude
Of upright souls be mine.

"Let winds that blow from heaven refresh,
Dear Lord, the languid air;
And let the weakness of the flesh
Thy strength of spirit share.

"And, if the eye must fail of light,
The ear forget to hear,
Make clearer still the spirit's sight,
More fine the inward ear!

"Be near me in mine hours of need
To soothe, or cheer, or warn,
And down these slopes of sunset lead
As up the hills of morn!"

It is safe to say that no other American poet, and perhaps no other poet of this age, has painted his own career with such absolute truthfulness, or weighed himself in a balance so delicate.

CHAPTER XI

EARLY LOVES AND LOVE POETRY

It is hard to associate with the Whittier of maturer years a passage like this written from Boston in 1829, at the age of twenty-three; —

"Here I have been all day trying to write something for my paper, but what with habitual laziness, and a lounge or two in the Athenæum Gallery, I am altogether unfitted for composition. . . . There are a great many pretty girls at the Athenæum, and I like to sit there and remark upon the different figures that go flitting by me, like aerial creatures just stooping down to our dull earth, to take a view of the beautiful creations of the painter's genius. I love to watch their airy motions, notice the dark brilliancy of their fine eyes, and observe the delicate flush stealing over their cheeks, but, trust me, my heart is untouched, — cold and motionless as a Jutland lake lighted up by the moonshine. I always did love a pretty girl. Heaven grant there is no harm in it! . . . Mr. Garrison will deliver an address on the Fourth of July. He goes to see his Dulcinea every other night almost, but is fearful of being 'shipped off,' after all, by her. Lord help the poor fellow, if it happens so. I like my business very well; but hang me if I like the people here. I am acquainted with a few girls, and have no wish to be so with many."[1]

Mr. Pickard however assures us that there are many similar passages in Whittier's early letters; and this boyish semi-sentimentalism, even if it reaches the confines of romance, has really no more perilous quality of

[1] Pickard's "Whittier," I. 93-4.

passion than has Whittier's equally unexpected "Hang me!" of profanity. What we know about the maturer Whittier is that no man has touched in a higher and simpler strain the images of beauty and the associations of youthful love.

Perhaps the nearest we shall ever come to his own habitual views of matrimony as a personal application may be found in his reply to a young girl with whom he was fond of talking, and who once replied, —

> "'Mr. Whittier, you often ask me to tell you about my experiences; I think you ought to tell me about yours.'
>
> "'Well,' said the poet, 'it isn't likely, Mary, that one has lived so long as I have in the world without having had some experiences, but it isn't worth while for an old man to talk much about them. Time was when I had my dreams and fancies — but those days have long since passed — don't thee think I should have made a pretty good husband?'
>
> "'Yes,' said Mary; 'but I think if thee had wished to go to Amesbury on a certain train thee would have gone, wife or no wife.'"

At which he laughed a merry laugh, vigorously smote his knee, and said, "I guess thee is about right, Mary."[1]

Yet in reading the memoirs of poets it is impossible not to find the basis of their early inspirations, three times out of four, in some personal experience of love and romance. It is, on the other hand, an inconvenience of lifelong bachelorhood that innumerable stories arise about a man, first and last; and that however shy his personal relations with women, he only gives the more place for supposed wanderings of the heart. Whittier's elder sister, looking back from middle life, could find nothing positive to tell me of any such

[1] Claflin's "Reminiscences," p. 68.

wanderings in his case, and could only say that there had been vague reports, to which she attached no value, about "somebody at Amesbury." The *Century Magazine* for May, 1902, contained what was called "a noteworthy letter" by Whittier, edited by Mr. William Lyon Phelps and addressed to Miss Cornelia Russ of Hartford, Conn., on his leaving that city on Dec. 31, 1831. It contains a proposal of an interview, apparently with a view to marriage. Mr. Pickard, his literary editor, frankly doubts the genuineness of this letter, and partly from its signature, "Yours most truly," a loss of the Quaker form which has not other example among his early correspondence; and he also questions the correctness of its dates, because he finds Whittier to have left Hartford permanently several months earlier than the date of the letter. He also disapproves, apparently, the assumption of Mr. Phelps that the object of this letter was the person who inspired that poem of Whittier which came nearest to a love-song, "Memories." He asserts positively that the real object of this poem was a lady of whom Mr. Pickard thus writes in a newspaper communication since the publication of his volume.

"She died several years ago, the widow of Judge Thomas of Covington, Ky. She was born in Haverhill, and was a distant relative of Whittier's, her maiden name being Mary Emerson Smith. Her grandmother, Mrs. Nehemiah Emerson, was a second cousin of Whittier's father. As a girl she was often at her grandfather Emerson's, and Whittier as a boy lived for a time at the same place, and attended school in that district. He called Mary's grandmother "Aunt." Afterward they were fellow students at Haverhill Academy. When Whittier was editing the *American*

Manufacturer, in Boston, she was at a seminary at Kennebunk, Me., and they were in correspondence, which showed a warm attachment on his part. I have seen the originals of these letters. There were several considerations which forbade thought of marriage on the part of either of them. She went to Cincinnati with her uncles, about 1831, and for this reason he planned to go West in 1832, but was prevented by a prospect of being elected to Congress from the Essex district. Up to the time of her marriage to Judge Thomas, Whittier's letters to her were frequent, all written in a brotherly tone, and giving the gossip of Haverhill. In one letter, written in 1832, he refers to his just published poem, 'Moll Pitcher,' and says he has in it drawn a portrait of herself. This portrait may be found on pages 26, 27, of the poem, and it is probable that the reason why 'Moll Pitcher' does not appear in any collection of his works is that he used several passages of it in other and later poems. Thus, the first stanza of 'Memories' is copied almost verbatim from these lines in 'Moll Pitcher': —

"'A beautiful and sylph-like girl,
With step as soft as summer air—
With fresh, young lip and brow of pearl,
Shadowed by many a natural curl
Of unconfined and flowing hair—
With the moist eye of pitying care,
Is bending like a seraph there:
A seeming child in everything
Save in her ripening maiden charms;
As nature wears the smile of spring,
When sinking into summer's arms.'

"It will be noticed that the person described in 'Memories' is remembered as a child, and this does not apply to the case of Miss Russ, as it does apply to Miss Smith. Then again, the 'hazel eyes' and 'brown tresses' belong to Miss Smith, and not, as I have understood, to the Hartford lady."

Apart from these boyish traditions, the person with whom Whittier's name was most persistently attached, in the way of matrimonial predictions, was an accomplished and attractive person named Elizabeth Lloyd, whom he knew intimately in Friends' Meeting, though she afterward became, like many of the Philadelphia Friends, an Episcopalian. She, like himself, printed many poems, one of which gave her a sort of vicarious celebrity, being that entitled "Milton's Prayer in Blindness," which was taken by many to be a real production of the poet. I can well remember to have heard this theory defended by cultivated people; and the impression so far prevailed, that it was understood to have been reprinted in an English edition of Milton's "Works." I remember well this lady at a later period during her widowhood, as Mrs. Howell; she had the remains of beauty, was dainty in her person and dress, and was very agreeable in conversation. She was invariably described as having been a personal friend of Whittier's, and was unquestionably the person mentioned by him in his poem called originally "An Incident among the White Mountains," but more recently "Mountain Pictures, Monadnock from Wachusett."[1] In later years, I fear, she was not quite loyal to his memory; and was known to criticise him as rustic, untravelled, without various experience; but she must remain in the world's memory, if at all, like so many Italian women in the past, as the possible retrospective candidate for the glory of a poet's early love.

However this may be, it is deeply interesting to trace, through Whittier's earlier and later poems, this dawning of pure and high emotion. We find it first,

[1] "Works," II. 57.

in one of his best known poems; that which Matthew Arnold recognised as "one of the perfect poems, which must live"[1]: —

"Still sits the schoolhouse by the road,
 A ragged beggar sleeping;
Around it still the sumachs grow,
 And blackberry vines are creeping.

"Within, the master's desk is seen,
 Deep-scarred by raps official;
The warping floor, the battered seats,
 The jack-knife's carved initial;

"The charcoal frescos on the wall;
 It's door's worn sill, betraying
The feet that, creeping slow to school,
 Went storming out to playing!

"Long years ago a winter sun
 Shone over it at setting;
Lit up its western window-panes,
 And low eves' icy fretting.

"It touched the tangled golden curls,
 And brown eyes full of grieving
Of one who still her steps delayed
 When all the school were leaving.

"For near her stood the little boy
 Her childish favour singled,
His cap pulled low upon a face
 Where pride and shame were mingled.

"Pushing with restless feet the snow
 To right and left he lingered, —
As restlessly her tiny hands
 The blue-checked apron fingered.

[1] Mrs. Fields's "Whittier," p. 65.

"He saw her lift her eyes, he felt
The soft hand's light caressing,
And heard the tremble of her voice,
As if a fault confessing.

"'I'm sorry that I spelt the word;
I hate to go above you:
Because,' — the brown eyes lower fell —
'Because, you see, I love you.'

"Still memory to a gray-haired man
That sweet child-face is showing.
Dear girl! the grasses on her grave
Have forty years been growing."

I withhold the closing verse with its moral; a thing always hard for Whittier to forego.

The next example of Whittier's range of love poetry is to be found in that exquisite romance of New England life and landscape, known as "My Playmate," of which Tennyson said justly to Mrs. Maria S. Porter, "It is a perfect poem; in some of his descriptions of scenery and wild flowers, he would rank with Wordsworth." It interprets the associations around him and the dreams of the long past as neither Longfellow, nor Lowell, nor Holmes, could have done it; the very life of life in love-memories in the atmosphere where he was born and dwelt. Many a pilgrim has sought the arbutus at Follymill or listened to the pines on Ramoth Hill with as much affection as he would seek the haunts of Chaucer; and has felt anew the charm of the association, the rise and fall of the simple music, the skill of the cadence, the way the words fall into place, the unexplained gift by which this man who could scarcely tell one tune from another on the piano became musical by instinct when innocent early memories swayed him. Note that in the whole sixteen verses the great majority of the words are monosyllables; observe how the veeries sing themselves into the line; and how the moaning of the sea of change rushes out and prolongs itself until the revery is passed, and the same sea sweeps in and ends the dream as absolutely as that one whirling cloud of disastrous air, from the St. Pierre volcano, ended every breath of mortal life for thirty-six thousand human beings. See, again, how in the fourth verse, out of twenty-six words, every one is made monosyllabic in order that the one word "bashful" may linger and be effective; and see how in the sixth the one long word in the whole poem "uneventful" multiplies indefinitely those bereft and solitary years. Did Whittier plan those effects deliberately? Probably not, but they are there; and the most exquisite combination of sounds in Tennyson or in Mrs. Browning's "Sonnets from the Portuguese," can only equal them. Even to Whittier, they came only in a favoured hour; and in the more continuous test of blank verse, he fails, like every modern poet since Keats, save Tennyson, alone.

"Amy Wentworth" is also one of his very best, and has the same delicate precision of sound to the ear and in the use of proper names; the house in Jaffrey Street, with its staircase and its ivy; with Elliot's green bowers and the sweet-brier, blooming on Kittery side—the very name "side" being local. This, however, was a wholly fictitious legend, as he himself told me; and still more imaginative was his last ballad, written at the age of sixty-eight, which I quote, in preference to "My Playmate," as less known. It has the peculiar interest of having been written in answer to a challenge coming from a young lady who said to him while they were staying together at his favourite Bearcamp River, "Mr. Whittier, you never wrote a love-song. I would like to have you try to write one for me to sing." The next day he handed her the following, and she was the first person to set it to music and sing it. He evidently worked it over afterward, however, for it must have been written at the earliest in the summer of 1876, was offered to the *Atlantic Monthly* in February, 1877, with some expressions of doubtful confidence; was withdrawn by the author, and was finally published in the *Independent* in Dec. 20, 1877, with this prose letter accompanying —

"I send, in compliance with the wish of Mr. Bowen and thyself, a ballad upon which, though not long, I have bestowed a good deal of labour. It is not exactly a Quakerly piece, nor is it didactic, and it has no moral that I know of. But it is, I think, *natural*, simple, and not unpoetical."

Here is the ballad with its Elizabethan flavour: a ballad written at nearly three-score-and-ten, upon a day's notice: —

THE HENCHMAN

"My lady walks her morning round,
My lady's page her fleet greyhound;
My lady's hair the fond winds stir
And all the birds make songs for her.

"Her thrushes sing in Rathburn bowers,
And Rathburn's side is gay with flowers;
But ne'er like hers, in flower or bird,
Was beauty seen or music heard.

"The distance of the stars is hers;
The least of all her worshippers,
The dust beneath her dainty heel,
She knows not that I see or feel.

"O proud and calm! she cannot know
Where'er she goes with her I go:
O cold and fair! she cannot guess
I kneel to share her hound's caress.

"Gay knights beside her hunt and hawk,
I rob their ears of her sweet talk;
Her suitors come from east and west,
I steal her smiles from every guest.

"Unheard of her, in loving words
I greet her with the song of birds;
I reach her with her green-armed bowers,
I kiss her with the lips of flowers.

"The hound and I are on her trail,
The wind and I uplift her veil;
As if the calm cool moon she were,
And I the tide, I follow her.

"As unrebuked as they, I share
The license of the sun and air,
And in a common homage hide
My worship from her scorn and pride.

"World-wide apart, and yet so near,
I breathe her charmed atmosphere,
Wherein to her my service brings
The reverence due to holy things.

"Her maiden pride, her haughty name,
My dumb devotion shall not shame;
The love that no return doth crave
To knightly level lifts the slave.

"No lance have I, in joust or fight
To splinter in my lady's sight;
But at her feet how blest were I
For any need of hers to die."

When in his later years, he had matured the ballad measure, he gives us also something which, as an English critic, Mr. W. J. Linton, has said "reads as if it might be from the old French, or a ballad which Dante Rossetti might have written": —

THE SISTERS

"Annie and Rhoda, sisters twain,
Woke in the night to the sound of rain,

"The rush of wind, the ramp and roar,
Of great waves climbing a rocky shore.

"Annie rose up in her bedgown white,
And looked out into the storm and night.

"'Hush, and hearken!' she cried in fear,
'Hearest thou nothing? sister dear!'

"'I hear the sea and the plash of rain,
And roar of the northeast hurricane.

"'Get thee back to the bed so warm!
No good comes of watching a storm.

"'What is it to thee, I fain would know,
That waves are roaring and wild winds blow?

"'No lover of thine is afloat to miss
The harbour lights on a night like this.'

"'But I heard a voice cry out my name:
Up from the sea on the wind it came.

"'Twice and thrice have I heard it call;
And the voice is the voice of Estwick Hall.'

"On the pillow the sister tossed her head :
'Hall of the Heron is safe,' she said.

"'In the tautest schooner that ever swam
He rides at anchor in Anisquam.

"'And, if in peril from swamping sea
Or lee-shore rocks, would he call on thee ?'

"But the girl heard only the wind and tide,
And wringing her small white hands she cried —

"'O sister Rhoda ! there's something wrong :
I hear it again, so loud and long.

"'"Annie ! Annie !" I hear it call,
And the voice is the voice of Estwick Hall.'

"Up sprang the elder with eyes aflame ;
'Thou liest ! he never would call thy name,

"'If he did, I would pray the wind and sea
To keep him for ever from thee and me.'

"Then out of the sea blew a dreadful blast :
Like the cry of a dying man it passed.

"The young girl hushed on her lips a groan,
But through her tears a strange light shone —

"The solemn joy of her heart's release
To own and cherish its love in peace.

"'Dearest !' she whispered under breath,
'Life was a lie, but true is death.

"'The love I hid from myself away
Shall crown me now in the light of day.

"'My ears shall never to wooer list,
Never by lover my lips be kissed.

" 'Sacred to thee am I henceforth,
Thou in heaven and I on earth.'

" She came and stood by her sister's bed;
'Hall of the Heron is dead!' she said.

" 'The winds and the waves their work have done,
We shall see him no more beneath the sun.

" 'Little will reck that heart of thine,
It loved him not with a love like mine.

" 'I for his sake, were he but here,
Could hem and broider thy bridal gear;

" 'Though hands should tremble and eyes be wet,
And stitch for stitch in my heart be set.

" 'But now my soul with his soul I wed;
Thine the living and mine the dead.' "

This is in the highest degree dramatic, but the traces of individual feeling come back to us most deeply, after all, in the personal lyrics, like the following, behind which some direct private experience must, unquestionably, have stood:—

MEMORIES

" How thrills once more the lengthening chain
Of memory at the thought of thee!
Old hopes which long in dust have lain,
Old dreams come thronging back again,
And boyhood lives again in me:
I feel its glow upon my cheek.
Its fulness of the heart is mine,
As when I leaned to hear thee speak,
Or raised my doubtful eye to thine.

"I hear again thy low replies,
I feel thy arm within my own,
And timidly again uprise
The fringèd lids of hazel eyes
With soft brown tresses overblown.
Ah! memories of sweet summer eves,
Of moonlit wave and willowy way,
Of stars and flowers and dewy leaves,
And smiles and tones more dear than they!

"Ere this thy quiet eye hath smiled
My picture of thy youth to see,
When, half a woman, half a child,
Thy very artlessness beguiled,
And folly's self seemed wise in thee.
I, too, can smile when o'er that hour
The lights of memory backward stream,
Yet feel the while that manhood's power
Is vainer than my boyhood's dream.

"Years have passed on, and left their trace,
Of graver care and deeper thought;
And unto me the calm, cold face
Of manhood, and to thee the grace
Of woman's pensive beauty brought.
More wide, perchance, for blame than praise,
The schoolboy's humble name has flown;
Thine, in the green and quiet ways
Of unobtrusive goodness known.

"And wider yet in thought and deed
Diverge our pathways, one in youth;
Thine the Genevan's sternest creed,
While answers to my spirit's need
The Derby dalesman's simple truth.
For thee, the priestly rite and prayer,
And holy day, and solemn psalm;
For me, the silent reverence where
My brethren gather, slow and calm.

"Yet hath thy spirit left on me
An impress Time has worn not out,
And something of myself in thee,
A shadow from the past, I see,
Lingering, even yet, thy way about;
Not wholly can the heart unlearn
That lesson of its better hours,
Nor yet has Time's dull footstep worn
To common dust the path of flowers."

CHAPTER XII

WHITTIER THE POET

In passing from the domain of love poetry and considering Whittier's more general claims as a poet, we must accept Lord Bacon's fine definition of poetry that "It hath something divine in it, because it raises the mind and hurries it into sublimity, by conforming the shows of things to the desires of the soul, instead of subjecting the soul to external things, as reason and history do." In this noble discrimination, — which one wonders not to have been cited among the rather inadequate arguments to prove that Lord Bacon was the real Shakespeare, — we have the key, so far as there is any, for the change from the boy Whittier, with his commonplace early rhymes, into the man who reached the sublime anthem of "My Soul and I." He also was "hurried into sublimity."

In the case of Holmes, it is a very common remark that his prose, especially "The Autocrat of the Breakfast Table," will outlast his poems, except perhaps "The Chambered Nautilus." No one can make any similar suggestion in regard to Whittier, whose best poetry wholly surpasses his best prose, in respect to grasp and permanence. It is, indeed, rather surprising to see how much of his prose he has thought it best to preserve, and by how little literary distinction it is marked. Earnestness and sound sense, it always has; and it always throws its stress on the side of manly sympathy and human progress, but more than this cannot be said. His few attempts at fiction are without marked life, and the little poems interspersed in them are better than the prose, which is rarely the case with authors. Much of this prose is simply in the line of reformatory journalism, and does not bear the test of the bound volume. Even in his narratives of real experience there is nothing to be compared with Lowell's "Moosehead Journal," or in general literary merit with his "On a Certain Condescension in Foreigners." On the other hand, Whittier escapes the pitfalls or tiresome side-paths into which both Lowell and Holmes were sometimes tempted; he may be prosaic, but never through levity, as sometimes happened to Lowell, or through some scientific whim, as in case of Holmes; and though his prose never has, on the literary side, the affluence of "Hyperion," it never shows the comparative poverty of "Kavanagh." It is, nevertheless, as a whole, so far inferior to his poems, that it is best at this day to give our chief attention to these.

No one can dwell much on Whittier without recognising him as the distinctively American poet of familiar life. More than any other he reaches the actual existence of the people, up to the time of his death. He could say of himself what Lowell said dramatically only, "We draw our lineage from the oppressed." Compared with him Longfellow, Holmes, and even Lowell, seem the poets of a class; Whittier alone is near the people; setting apart Emerson, who inhabited a world of his own, "so near and yet so far." His whole position was indeed characteristic of American society; had he lived in England, he would always have been, at his highest, in the position of some Corn-Law Rhymer, some Poet of the People; or at best, in the often degrading position of his favourite Burns himself, whereas in his own country this external difference was practically forgotten. Having gone thus far in fitting out this modest poet, nature gave to him, more directly than to either of the others, the lyric gift—a naturalness of song and flow, increasing with years and reaching where neither of the others attained. A few of Longfellow's poems have this, but Whittier it pervades; and beginning like Burns, with the very simplest form, the verse of four short lines, he gradually trained himself, like Burns, to more varied or at least to statelier measures.

Burns was undoubtedly his literary master in verse and Milton in prose. He said of Burns to Mrs. Fields, "He lives, next to Shakespeare, in the heart of humanity."[1] His contentment in simple measures was undoubtedly a bequest from this poet and was carried even farther, while his efforts were more continuous in execution and higher in tone. On the other hand, he drew from Milton his long prose sentences and his tendency to the florid rather than the terse. His conversation was terse enough, but not his written style. He said to Mrs. Fields: "Milton's prose has long been my favourite reading. My whole life has felt the influence of his writings."[2] He once wrote to Fields that Allingham, after Tennyson, was his favourite among modern British poets. I do not remember him as

[1] Fields's "Whittier," p. 51.
[2] Fields's "Whittier," p. 41.

quoting Browning or speaking of him. This may, however, have been an accident.

One of the very ablest of New England critics, a man hindered only by prolonged ill-health from taking a conspicuous leadership, David Atwood Wasson, himself the author of that noble poem with its seventeenth-century flavour, "All's Well," wrote in 1864 in the *Atlantic Monthly* what is doubtless the profoundest study of Whittier's temperament and genius. From this I gladly quote some passages: —

"It was some ten years ago," he writes, "that we first met John Greenleaf Whittier, the poet of the moral sentiment and of the heart and faith of the people of America. It chanced that we had been making notes, with much interest, upon the genius of the Semitic nations. That peculiar simplicity, centrality, and intensity which caused them to originate Monotheism from two independent centres, the only systems of pure Monotheism which have had power in history, while the same characteristics made their poetry always lyrical, never epic or dramatic, and their most vigorous thought a perpetual sacrifice on the altars of the will, this had strongly impressed us; and we seemed to find in it a striking contrast to the characteristic genius of the Aryan or Indo-Germanic nations, with their imaginative interpretations of the religious sentiment, with their epic and dramatic expansions, and their taste for breadth and variety. Somewhat warm with these notions we came to a meeting with our poet, and the first thought on seeing him was — 'The head of a Hebrew prophet!' It is not Hebrew — Saracen rather — the Jewish type is heavier, more material; but it corresponded strikingly to the conceptions we had formed of the Southern Semitic crania, and the whole make of the man was of the same character. The high cranium, so lofty, especially in the dome — the slight and symmetrical backward slope of the whole head — the powerful level brows, and beneath these the dark, deep eyes, so full of shadowed fire — the Arabian complexion — the sharp-cut, intense lines of the face — the light, tall, erect stature — the quick axial poise of the movement — all these answered with singular accuracy to the picture of those preacher-races which had been shaping itself in our imagination. Indeed the impression was so strong as to induce some little feeling of embarrassment. It seemed slightly awkward and insipid to be meeting a prophet here in a parlour and in a spruce masquerade of modern costume, shaking hands, and saying, 'Happy to meet you!' after the fashion of our feeble civilities.

"All this came vividly to remembrance on taking up, the other day, Whittier's last book of poems — 'In War-time' — a volume that has been welcomed all over the land with enthusiastic delight. Had it been no more, however, than a mere personal reminiscence, it should, at present, have remained private. But have we not here a key to Whittier's genius? Is not this Semitic centrality and simplicity, this prophetic depth, reality, and vigour, without great lateral and intellectual range, its especial characteristic? He has not the liberated, light-winged Greek imagination — imagination not involved and included in the religious sentiment, but playing in epic freedom and with various interpretation between religion and intellect — he has not the flowing, Protean, imaginative sympathy, the power of instant self-identification, with all forms of character and life which culminated in Shakespeare; but that imaginative vitality which lurks in faith and conscience, producing what we may call *ideal force of heart.* This he has eminently; and it is this central, invisible, Semitic heat which makes him a poet. Imagination exists in him, not as a separable faculty, but as a pure vital suffusion. Hence he is an *inevitable* poet. There is no drop of his blood, there is no fibre of his brain, which does not crave poetical expression. . . ."

Mr. Edmund Clarence Stedman, a recognised authority on American poetry, says admirably of Whittier: —

". . . His imperfections were those of his time and class. He never learned compression, and still [1885] is troubled more with fatal fluency than our other poets of equal rank, — by an inability to reject poor stanzas and to stop at the right place. But there came a period when his verse was composed with poetic intent, and after a less careless fashion. . . . 'Cassandra Southwick,' alone, showed where his strength lay; of all our poets he is the most natural balladist. . . . And as a bucolic poet of his own section, rendering its pastoral life and aspect, Whittier surpasses all rivals. . . . Longfellow's rural pieces were done by a skilled workman, who could regard his themes objectively and put them to good use. Lowell delights in out-door life, and his Yankee studies are perfect; still we feel that he is intellectually and socially miles above the people of the vales. Whittier is of their blood, and always the boy-poet of the Essex farm, however advanced in years and fame. They are won by the sincerity and ingenuousness of his verse, rooted in the soil and nature as the fern and wild-rose of the wayside. . . . He himself despises a sham pastoral. There is good criticism, a clear sense of what is needed, in his paper on Robert Dinsmore, the old Scotch bard of his childhood. He says of rural poetry that 'the mere dilettante and the amateur ruralist may as well keep their hands off. The prize is not for them. He who would successfully strive for it must be himself the thing he sings, one who has added to his book-lore the large experience of an active participation in the rugged toil, the hearty amusements, the trials and pleasures he describes.'"

"Whittier's origin and early life," writes Stedman, "were auspicious for one who was to become a poet of the people. His muse shielded him from the relaxing influence of luxury and superfine culture. These could not reach the primitive homestead in the beautiful Merrimac Valley, five miles out from the market-town of Haverhill, where all things were elementary and of the plainest cast. The training of the Friends made his boyhood more simple, otherwise it mattered little whether he derived from Puritan or Quaker sources. Still it was much, in one respect, to be descended from Quakers and Huguenots used to suffer and be strong for conscience' sake. It placed him years in advance of the comfortable Brahmin class, with its blunted sense of right and wrong, and, to use his own words, turned him 'so early away from what Roger Williams calls the world's great trinity, pleasure, profit, and honour, to take side with the poor and oppressed.' . . . Whittier's Quaker strain yielded him wholly to the 'intellectual passion.' That transcendentalism aroused, and still keeps him obedient to the Inward Light. And it made him a poet militant, a crusader, whose moral weapons, since he must disown the carnal, were keen of edge and seldom in their scabbards. The fire of his deep-set eyes, whether betokening, like that of his kinsman Webster, the Batchelder blood, or inherited from some old Feuillevert, strangely contrasts with the benign expression of his mouth, — that firm serenity which by transmitted habitude dwells upon the lips of the sons and daughters of peace.

"There was no affectation in the rusticity of his youth. It was the real thing, the neat and saving homeliness of the eastern farm. . . . Of our leading poets he was almost the only one who learned Nature by working with her at all seasons, under the sky and in the wood.

". . . But the mission of his life now came upon him. It was no personal ambition that made him the psalmist of the new movement. His verses, crude as they were, had gained favour; he already had a name, and a career was predicted for him. He now doomed himself to years of retardation and disfavour, and had no reason to foresee the honours they would bring him in the end. What he tells us is the truth: 'For twenty years my name would have injured the circulation of any of the literary or political journals of the country.' . . . Bryant, many years later, pointed out that in recent times the road of others to literary success had been made smooth by antislavery opinions, adding that in Whittier's case the reverse of that was true; that he made himself the champion of the slave, 'when to say aught against the national curse was to draw upon one's self the bitterest hatred, loathing, and contempt, of the great majority of men throughout the land.' Unquestionably, Whittier's ambition, during his novitiate, had been to do something as a poet and a man of letters. Not that he had learned what few in fact at that time realised, that the highest art aims at creative beauty, and that devotion, repose, and calm, are essential to the mastery of an ideal. . . . We measure poetry at its worth, not at the worth of the maker. This is the law; yet in Whittier's record, if ever, there is an appeal to the higher law that takes note of exceptions. Some of his verse, as a pattern for verse hereafter, is not what it might have been if he had consecrated himself to poetry as an art; but it is memorably connected with historic times, and his rudest shafts of song were shot true and far and tipped with flame. . . . His songs touched the hearts of his people. It was the generation which listened in childhood to the 'Voices of Freedom,' that fulfilled their prophecies. . . .

"After the war, Garrison, at last crowned with honour, and rejoicing in the consummation of his work, was seldom heard. Whittier, in his hermitage, the resort of many pilgrims, as steadily renewed his song."

The poem in which Stedman finds the highest claim to have been made by Whittier as a natural balladist is the following:—

CASSANDRA SOUTHWICK

It is a story of 1658, of a young Quaker girl sentenced in Boston, for her religion, to be transported to Virginia, and there sold as a slave. She is brought from prison to where the merchant ships are at anchor, and the ship-men are asked who will take charge of her.

This is what follows:—

"But gray heads shook and young brows knit the while the sheriff read
That law the wicked rulers against the poor have made.

* * * * * * *

"Grim and silent stood the captains, and when again he cried,
'Speak out, my worthy seamen!' no voice, no sign replied;

"But I felt a hard hand press my own, and kind words met my ear:
'God bless thee, and preserve thee, my gentle girl and dear!'

"A weight seemed lifted from my heart, a pitying friend was nigh;
I felt it in his hard rough hand, and saw it in his eye;

"And when again the Sheriff spoke, that voice so kind to me
Growled back its stormy answer, like the roaring of the sea.

"'Pile my ship with bars of silver, pack with coins of Spanish gold
From keel-piece up to deck-plank the roomage of her hold,

"'By the living God who made me, I would sooner in your bay
Sink ship and crew and cargo than bear this child away!'

"'Well answered, worthy captain! shame on their cruel laws!'
Ran through the crowd in murmurs loud the people's just applause.

"'Like the herdsmen of Tekoa, in Israel of old,
Shall we see the poor and righteous again for silver sold?'

"I looked on haughty Endicott with weapon half-way drawn,
Swept round the throng his lion glare of bitter hate and scorn;

"Fiercely he drew his bridle-rein and turned in silence back,
And sneering priest and baffled clerk rode murmuring in his track.

"Hard after them the Sheriff looked, in bitterness of soul;
Thrice smote his staff upon the ground, and crushed his parchment roll.

"'Good friends!' he said, 'since both have fled, the ruler and the priest,
Judge ye, if from their farther work I be not well released.'

"Loud was the cheer which full and clear swept round the silent bay,
As with kind words and kinder looks, he bade me go my way:

"For He who turns the courses of the streamlet of the glen
And the river of great waters, had turned the hearts of men."

It was a natural result of his reticent habit and retired life that his maturer poems impress us, as we dwell upon them, with more sense of surprise as to their origin and shaping than exists in the case of any of his compeers, save only the almost equally reticent Emerson. In Longfellow's memoirs, in Lowell's letters, we see them discussing their purposes with friends, accepting suggestion and correction, while Whittier's poems come always with surprise, and even Mr. Pickard's careful labours add little to our knowledge. Mrs. Claflin and Mrs. Fields give us little as to the actual origins of his poems. I have never felt this deficiency more than in sitting in his house, once or twice, since his death, and observing the scantiness of even his library. Occasional glimpses in his notes help us a very little, as for instance what he says in the preface to his "Child Life in Prose," published in 1873, as to his early sources of inspiration: —

"It is possible that the language and thought of some portions of the book may be considered beyond the comprehension of the class for which it is intended. Admitting that there may be truth in the objection, I believe, with Coventry Patmore in his preface to a child's book, that the charm of such a volume is increased rather than lessened by the surmised existence of an unknown element of power, meaning, and beauty. I well remember how, at a very early age, the solemn organ-roll of Gray's 'Elegy' and the lyric sweep and pathos of Cowper's 'Lament for the Royal George' moved and fascinated me with a sense of mystery and power felt rather than understood. 'A spirit passed before my face, but the form thereof was not discerned.' Freighted with unguessed meanings, these poems spake to me, in an unknown tongue, indeed, but like the wind in the pines or the waves on the beach, awakening faint echoes and responses, and vaguely prophesying of wonders yet to be revealed."

He was the Tyrtaeus or leading bard of the greatest moral movement of the age; and he probably gained in all ways from the strong tonic of the antislavery agitation. This gave a training in directness, simplicity, genuineness; it taught him to shorten his sword and to produce strong effects by common means. It made him permanently high-minded also, and placed him, as he himself always said, above the perils and temptations of a merely literary career. Though always careful in his work, and a good critic of the work of others, he usually talked by preference upon subjects not literary — politics, social science, the rights of labour. He would speak at times, if skilfully led up to it, about his poems, and was sometimes, though rarely, known to repeat them aloud; but his own personality was never a favourite theme with him, and one could easily fancy him as going to sleep, like La Fontaine, at the performance of his own opera.

In his antislavery poetry he was always simple, always free from that excess or over-elaborateness of metaphor to be seen sometimes in Lowell. On the other hand he does not equal Lowell in the occasional condensation of vigorous thought into great general maxims. Lowell's "Verses suggested by the Present Crisis" followed not long after Whittier's "Massachusetts to Virginia," and, being printed anonymously, was at first attributed to the same author. Whittier's poems had even more lyric fire and produced an immediate impression even greater, but it touched universal principles less broadly, and is therefore now rarely quoted, while Lowell's

"Truth forever on the scaffold, wrong forever on the throne,"

is immortal on the lips of successive orators.

Brought up at a period when Friends disapproved of music, Whittier had no early training in this direction, and perhaps no natural endowment. He wrote in a letter of 1882, — "I don't know anything of music, not one tune from another." This at once defined the limits of his verse, and restricted him to the very simplest strains. He wrote mostly in the four-line ballad metre, which he often made not only very effective, but actually melodious. That he had a certain amount of natural ear is shown by his use of proper names, in which, after his early period of Indian experiments had passed, he rarely erred. In one of his very best poems, "My Playmate," a large part of the effectiveness comes from the name of the locality: —

"The dark pines sing on Ramoth hill
The slow song of the sea."

He felt his own deficiency in regard to music, and had little faith in his own ear, the result being that even if he made a happy stroke in the way of sound, he was apt to distrust it at the suggestion of some prosaic friend with a foot rule, who convinced him that he was taking a dangerous liberty. Thus, in "The New Wife and the Old," in describing the night sounds, he finally closed with —

"And the great sea waves below,
Pulse o' the midnight beating slow."

This "pulse o' the midnight" was an unusual rhythmic

felicity for him, but, on somebody's counting the syllables, he tamely submitted, substituting

"Like the night's pulse, beating slow,"

which is spondaic and heavy; but he afterward restored the better line. In the same way, when he sang of the shoemakers in the very best of his "Songs of Labour," he originally wrote:—

"Thy songs, Hans Sachs, are living yet,
In strong and hearty German,
And Canning's craft and Gifford's wit,
And the rare good sense of Sherman."

Under similar pressure of criticism he was induced to substitute

"And patriot fame of Sherman,"

and this time he did not repent. It is painful to think what would have become of the liquid measure of Coleridge's "Christabel" had some tiresome acquaintance, possibly "a person on business from Porlock," insisted on thus putting that poem in the stocks.

It shows the essential breadth which lay beneath the religious training of the Society of Friends, even in its most conservative wing, that Whittier, not knowing a note of music, should have contributed more hymns to the hymn-book than any other poet of his time, although this is in many cases through the manipulation of others, which furnished results quite unexpected to him. In a collection of sixty-six hymns prepared for the Parliament of Religions at Chicago in 1893, more were taken from Whittier's poems than from any other author, these being nine in all. The volume edited by Longfellow and Johnson, called "Hymns of the

Spirit" (1864), has twenty-two from Whittier; the "Unitarian Hymn and Tune Book" of 1868, has seven, and Dr. Martineau's "Hymns of Praise" has seven. As has elsewhere been stated, Mr. and Mrs. Edwin D. Mead reported, after attending many popular meetings in England, in 1901, that they heard Whittier and Longfellow quoted and sung more freely than any other poets.

It is especially to be noticed that in Whittier's poems of the sea there is a salt breath, a vigorous companionship — perhaps because he was born and bred near it — not to be found in either of his companion authors. There is doubtless a dramatic movement, an onward sweep in Longfellow's "Wreck of the Hesperus" and "Sir Humphrey Gilbert" such as Whittier never quite attained, and the same may be true of the quiet, emotional touch in Longfellow's "The Fire of Driftwood"; nor was there ever produced in America, perhaps, any merely meditative poem of the sea so thoughtful and so perfect in execution as Holmes's "The Chambered Nautilus." Among American poets less known, Brownlee Brown's "Thalatta" and Helen Jackson's "Spoken" were respectively beyond him in their different directions. But for the daily atmosphere and life, not so much of the sea as of the seaside, for the companionship of the sailor, the touch that makes the ocean like a larger and more sympathetic human being to those who dwell within its very sound, Whittier stands before them all; he is simply a companion to the sailor, as he is to the farmer and the hunter; and he weaves out of the life of each a poetry such as its actual child hardly knows. The "Tent on the Beach" will always keep us nearer to the actual life of salt water than can anything by Whittier's companion poets.

Probably no poet was ever more surprised by the success of a new book than was Whittier by that of this poem about which, as he wrote to a friend, he had great misgivings, as it was prepared under especial disadvantages. He was amazed when he saw in the *Boston Transcript* that a first edition of ten thousand copies had been printed, and thought it "an awful swindle" upon the public that a thousand copies a day should have been sold. This made more striking the fact that he put into it, perhaps, the best bit of self-delineation he ever accomplished in the following lines: —

"And one there was, a dreamer born,
Who, with a mission to fulfil,
Had left the Muses' haunts to turn
The crank of an opinion mill,
Making his rustic reed of song
A weapon in the war with Wrong,
Yoking his fancy to the breaking plough
That beam-deep turned the soil for truth to spring and grow.

"Too quiet seemed the man to ride
The winged Hippogriff, Reform;
Was his a voice from side to side
To pierce the tumult of the storm?
A silent, shy, peace-loving man,
He seemed no fiery partisan
To hold his way against the public frown,
The ban of Church and State, the fierce mob's hounding down.

"For while he wrought with strenuous will
The work his hands had found to do,
He heard the fitful music still
Of winds that out of dreadland blew;

> The din about him could not drown
> What the strange voices whispered down ;
> Along his task-field weird processions swept,
> The visionary pomp of stately phantoms stepped."

The uncertainty of an author's judgment of his own books was never better illustrated than by the fact that Whittier's poem "Mabel Martin" first published under the name of "The Witch's Daughter" in the *National Era* for 1857 — erroneously described by Mr. Pickard as first published in 1866 — was his greatest immediate financial success. It was somewhat enlarged as "Mabel Martin" in 1877, and he received for it $1000 at the first annual payment. Mr. Pickard pronounces it "charming," but I suspect that it is rarely copied, and hardly ever quoted — perhaps because the three-line measure is unfavourable to Whittier's style or to the public tastes. The absence of rhyme from one line in each three-line verse is not compensated by any advantage, while the four-line verse of the dedication of the whole work to the memory of his mother is very attractive.

He has defects of execution which are easily apparent. His poems, even to the latest, are apt to be too long, and to be laden with a superfluous moral, and come dangerously near to meriting the criticism of D'Alembert on Richardson's long-winded words, once so lauded: "Nature is a good thing, but do not bore us with it (*non pas à l'ennui*)." Whittier did not actually reach the point of ennui, but came very near it. As for his rhymes, though not so bad as those of Elizabeth Barrett Browning, they were, in his early years, bad enough. Mr. Linton, from the English point of view, or from any other, was justified in protesting against such rhymes as *worn* and *turn*, *joins* and *pines*, *faults* and *revolts*, *flood* and *Hood*, *even* and *Devon*, *heaven* and *forgiven*.[1] We can easily find in addition, *mateless* and *greatness*, *pearl* and *marl*, *women* and *trimming*, *scamper* and *Hampshire*; some of all this list, it must be remembered, being mere archaisms or localisms, and all tending in Whittier's case, as in Mrs. Browning's, to entire disappearance after middle life. No one complains of the rhymes in "Sonnets from the Portuguese."

Even when Whittier uses a mispronunciation or makes a slip in grammar, it has the effect of oversight or of whim, rather than of ignorance. Thus he commonly accents the word "romance" on the first syllable, as in —

"Young Romance raised his dreamy eyes;"

while at other times he places the stress more correctly on the last, as where he writes —

"Where Tasso sang, let young Romance and Love."[2]

The only very conspicuous translation from Whittier into French, so far as I know, is one of his earliest poems called "The Vaudois Teacher"—first attributed to Mrs. Hemans — which was adopted as a local poem among the Waldenses, who did not know its origin until 1875, when the Rev. J. C. Fletcher communicated the fact to the Moderator of the Waldensian Synod, having himself heard the poem sung by students of D'Aubigné's seminary at Geneva. On Mr. Fletcher's return to Italy, in 1875, he caused the fact of authorship to be conveyed to the Synod, whose members rose

[1] Linton's "Whittier," p. 167.
[2] "Poetical Works," IV. 38.

and cheered and caused the Moderator to write a letter, of which the following is a translation — the letter being dated from Torré Pellicé, Piémont, Italie, September 13, 1875: —

"DEAR AND HONOURED BROTHER, — I have recently learned by a letter from my friend, J. C. Fletcher, now residing in Naples, that you are the author of the charming little poem, 'The Vaudois Colporteur,' which was translated several years ago in French by Professor de Felicé, of Montauban, and of which there is also an excellent Italian translation made by M. Giovanni Nicolini, Professor of our College at Torré Pellicé. There is not a single Vaudois who has received any education who cannot repeat from memory 'The Vaudois Colporteur' in French or in Italian. The members of the Synod of the Vaudois Church assembled to the number of about seventy at a pastoral banquet, on Thursday evening, the 9th inst., and unanimously voted the motion which I had the honour of proposing, viz.: That we should send a very warm Christian fraternal salutation to the author of 'The Vaudois Colporteur.' I was intrusted with the duty of conveying this salutation to you — a duty which I fulfil with joy, expressing at the same time our gratitude to you, and also our wish to receive, if possible, from yourself the original English, which is still unknown to us, of this piece of poetry, which we so justly prize. Accept, dear and honoured brother, these lines of respect and Christian love, from your sincere friend in the Lord Jesus,

"J. D. CHARBONNIER,
"Moderator of the Vaudois Church."

Mr. Whittier's reply, dated Amesbury, 10th mo., 21st, 1875, is in these words: —

"MY DEAR FRIEND, — I have received thy letter informing me of the generous appreciation of my little poem by the Synod of which thou art Moderator. Few events of my life have given me greater pleasure. I shall keep the letter amongst my most precious remembrances, and it will be a joy to me to know that in your distant country, and in those sanctuaries of the Alps, consecrated by such precious and holy memories, there are Christians, men and women, who think of me with kindness, and give me a place in their prayers. May the dear Lord and Father of us all keep you always under His protection."[1]

In summing up the results of Whittier's twin career as poet and as file-leader, it may be safely said that his early career of reformer made him permanently high-minded, and placed him above the perils and temptations of a merely literary career. This he himself recognised from the first, and wrote it clearly and musically in a poem printed at the very height of conflict (1847), more than ten years before the Civil War. He took this poem as the prelude to a volume published ten years later, and again while revising his poems for a permanent edition in 1892. Unlike many of his earlier compositions, it is reprinted by him without the change of a syllable.

"PROEM

"I love the old melodious lays
Which softly melt the ages through,
  The songs of Spenser's golden days,
  Arcadian Sidney's silvery phrase,
Sprinkling our noon of time with freshest morning dew.

"Yet vainly in my quiet hours
To breathe their marvellous notes I try;
  I feel them, as the leaves and flowers
  In silence feel the dewy showers,
And drink with glad still lips the blessing of the sky.

"The rigour of a frozen clime,
The harshness of an untaught ear,

[1] Pickard's "Whittier," II. 607-09.

The jarring words of one whose rhyme
Beat often Labour's hurried time
On Duty's rugged march through storm and strife, are here.

"Of mystic beauty, dreamy grace,
No rounded art the lack supplies;
Unskilled the subtler lines to trace
Or softer shades of Nature's face.
I view her common forms with unanointed eyes.

"Nor mine the seer-like power to show
The secrets of the heart and mind;
To drop the plummet-line below
Our common world of joy and woe,
A more intense despair or brighter hope to find.

"Yet here at least an earnest sense
Of human right and weal is shown,
A hate of tyranny intense
And hearty in its vehemence
As if my brother's pain and sorrow were my own.

"O Freedom! if to me belong
Nor mighty Milton's gift divine,
Nor Marvell's wit and graceful song,
Still, with a love as deep and strong
As theirs, I lay, like them, my best gifts on thy shrine."

It is well to close this chapter with these words he wrote, at the Asquam House, in 1882, on the death of Longfellow, in a copy of the latter's poems, belonging to my sister: —

"Hushed now the sweet consoling tongue
Of him whose lyre the Muses strung;
His last low swan-song had been sung!

"His last! And ours, dear friend, is near;
As clouds that rake the mountains here,
We too shall pass and disappear,

"Yet howsoever changed or tost,
Not even a wreath of mist is lost,
No atom can itself exhaust.

"So shall the soul's superior force
Live on and run its endless course
In God's unlimited universe.

"And we, whose brief reflections seem
To fade like clouds from lake and stream,
Shall brighten in a holier beam."

CHAPTER XIII

CLOSING YEARS

THERE was no literary man of his time who worked under such a lifelong embargo in respect to health as Whittier. He once said, "I inherited from my parents a nervous headache, and on account of it have never been able to do all I wished to do." Whittier's early trouble was regarded by physicians as a disease of the heart, and he was told that he must carefully avoid excitement. With care, as one of them assured him, he might live to be fifty years old. His headaches always pursued him, and he could not read continuously for half an hour without severe pain. At public dinners and receptions he was obliged to stipulate that he should be allowed to slip out when he felt fatigue coming on. It showed great strength of will surely for one man, combining the functions of author, politician, and general reformer, under such disadvantages, to outlive his fellow chiefs, carry so many points for which he had toiled, and leave behind him seven volumes of his collected works. The most successful of these, "Snow-bound," was written to beguile the weariness of a sick-chamber.

When editor of the *National Era* he wrote to Miss Wendell that he should have spent the winter in Washington but for the state of his health and the difficulty of leaving home on his mother's account. In the same letter (2d. mo. 21, 1847) he wrote: —

"I have of late been able to write but little, and that mostly for the papers, and I have scarcely answered a letter for a month past. I dread to touch a pen. Whenever I do it increases the dull wearing pain in my head, which I am scarcely ever free from."[1]

Yet at this time he was occasionally publishing eight or nine columns a week in the *National Era*, besides a large political correspondence.

"Sleep," says Mrs. Claflin, "was the one blessing that seemed to be denied him, and which he constantly longed for. He resorted to every simple remedy for insomnia — but it was all in vain — his was the 'sore disquiet of a restless brain,' and he would often come down in the morning looking tired and worn from his long night of wakefulness, and say, 'It is of no use; the sleep of the innocent is denied me. Perhaps I do not deserve it.'"[2]

While reticent and uncomplaining to strangers, we find him through life obliged to write to friends in such phrases as these, "I should have been glad to make Haverhill a visit in the winter, but the extremely delicate condition of my health has compelled me to forego that pleasure." "I now think some of going next week to New York and Philadelphia, partly to escape our east winds which I dread." "I think sickness has a wonderful effect in fanning into life the half-extinguished conscience. It is doubtless better for me and my friends that the hand of sickness is sometimes laid heavily upon me."

Being a bad sleeper, "seldom," as he said, "putting a solid bar of sleep between day and day," he habitually rose early and, as he claimed, "had rarely missed see-

[1] Pickard's "Whittier," I. 319.

[2] Claflin's "Personal Recollections," p. 40.

ing the sun rise for forty years." "I have lately felt great sympathy with ——,"[1] he said one morning, "for I have been kept awake one hundred and twenty hours; an experience I should not care to try again." He said also to Mrs. Fields: "I am forbidden to use my poor head, so I have to get along as I can without it. The Catholic St. Leon, thee knows, walked alert as usual after his head was cut off." "I cannot think very well of my own things," he elsewhere said to her; "and what is mere fame worth when thee is at home alone and sick with headaches, unable either to read or to write?" "He must often have known," adds this sympathetic friend, "the deeps of sadness in winter evenings, when he was too ill to touch book or pen, and when he could do nothing during the long hours but sit and think over the fire."

This loss of sleep and other unfavourable symptoms were by no means due to a sedentary life. His love of nature was deep and constant, and more like that of Emerson and Thoreau, than that of Longfellow and Lowell. He liked to be actually immersed in outdoor life, not merely to enjoy it as an episode. He loved to recall his first stay among the hills, when "his parents took him where he could see the great wooded slope of Agamenticus." "As he looked up and gazed with awe at the solemn sight, a cloud drooped, and hung suspended, as it were, from one point, and filled his soul with astonishment. He had never forgotten it. He said nothing at the time, but this cloud hanging from the breast of the hill, filled his boyish mind with a mighty wonder, which had never faded away."[2]

It was to ill health, I think, that his renunciation

[1] Fields's "Whittier," pp. 40, 59, 73. [2] *Ibid.*, p. 90.

of all far-off travel was due. He once told me, however, that perhaps the reason why he had never travelled, was that he had always been a great reader of books of travel, and after reading each one, had in his mind so vivid a picture of it that he wished to go somewhere else. What just ground have we to complain of this, when we know by Scott's own confession that his description of Melrose Abbey by moonlight, — one of the most widely quoted descriptions ever written, — was not written in presence of that beautiful spectacle, but quite the contrary? He wrote to Bernard Barton: —

"I was surprised into confessing what I might have as well kept to myself, that I had been guilty of sending persons a bat-hunting to see the ruins of Melrose by moonlight, which I never saw myself. The fact is rather curious, for as I have often slept nights at Melrose (when I did not reside so near the place), it is singular that I have not seen it by moonlight on some chance occasion. However, it so happens that I never did, and must (unless I get cold on purpose) be contented with supposing that these ruins look very like other Gothic buildings which I have seen by the wan light of the moon."[1]

This was carried so far by Whittier that during all his visits to the White Mountains, he never could be tempted to go to Quebec, but said, "I know all about it, by books and pictures, as if I had seen it." Yet how much he enjoyed thus tasting in imagination the atmosphere and the life of a foreign land, is to be seen in a charming picture given by him to Mrs. Fields of a talk with a wandering Arab whom he once encountered.

[1] "Letters and Poems of Bernard Barton," by his daughter, p. 147.

"'I was in my garden,' he said, 'when I saw an Arab wander down the street, and by-and-by stop and lean against my gate. He held a small book in his hand, which he was reading from time to time when he was not occupied with gazing about him. Presently I went to talk with him, and found he had lived all his life on the edge of the desert until he started for America. He was very homesick, and longed for the time of his return. He had hired himself for a term of years to the master of the circus. He held the Koran in his hand, and was delighted to find a friend who had also read his sacred book. He opened his heart still further then, and said how he longed for his old, wild life in the Desert, for a sight of the palms, and the sands, but above all for its freedom.'"[1]

It would be interesting to find out what effect Whittier's physical condition had upon the production of a work quite unique among his prose writings, "The Opium Eater," published in the *New England Magazine* in 1833, in his twenty-fourth year. He spoke of it to Fields and others as something which he had almost entirely forgotten. But it is preserved by him, nevertheless, in his works,[2] and certainly is, as he says, unique in respect to style. It is undoubtedly one of many similar productions coming from various pens and taking De Quincey's "Confessions of an Opium Eater" as their model, though this is really better than the average of such attempts. The question of interest is to know how far this literary experiment — evidently a deliberate thing, from its length and careful structure — was in any way the result of his illness, and, as such, a passing phenomenon only. "The Proselytes," published in the same year, and reprinted in the same volume, looks somewhat in the same morbid and unhealthy direction, from which the mass of Whittier's writings is so wholly free.

[1] Fields's "Whittier," p. 54. [2] "Works," I. 278.

Whittier's later years were calm and prosperous. He held no public position after his early service in the Massachusetts Legislature, but during the period when the overseers of Harvard College were chosen by the legislature he once served, in 1858, as overseer, and alluded to this jocosely in a letter to Lowell, then editor of the *Atlantic*, as giving him authority over Lowell. He received the Harvard honorary degree of Master of Arts in 1860, and that of Doctor of Laws in 1866, at the hundredth anniversary of the college, when he was the only literary man so decorated among a number of men of science, a fact which attracted some notice. He was made a trustee of Brown University (Providence, R.I.) in 1869. He was chosen a member of the Massachusetts Historical Society in 1863, and was borne upon its rolls for three years, but never accepted the office or even replied to the invitation, for some reason yet unexplained, so that his name was dropped. He declined membership of the Loyal Legion, a society of officers who had served on the Union side in the Civil War, and had a limited number of civilian members; but this he refused as an organisation inconsistent with the principles of the Society of Friends.

Whittier's seventieth birthday was celebrated more profusely than had happened to any American author before; and more so than was at first wholly congenial to his modest nature. The issue of a *Literary World* (Dec. 1, 1877), devoted to him wholly, on the part of various authors, he might have more easily endured; but the elaborate dinner given him by the publishers of the *Atlantic Monthly*, at Hotel Brunswick, in Boston, (Dec. 17, 1877) was an ordeal from which he is known to have greatly shrunk; and I can testify that this reluctance was quite visible in his face and manner. Mr. Houghton presided, and gave a history of the magazine, after which he introduced Whittier, who could do no less in return than make one of the very few brief speeches into which he found himself driven in later life. He said: —

"You must know you are not to expect a speech from me to-night. I can only say that I am very glad to meet with my friends of the *Atlantic*, a great many contributors to which I have only known through their writings, and that I thank them for the reception they have given me. When I supposed that I would not be able to attend this ceremony I placed in my friend Longfellow's hands a little bit of verse that I told him, if it were necessary, I wished he would read. My voice is of 'a timorous nature, and rarely to be heard above the breath.' Mr. Longfellow will do me the favour to read the writing. I shall be very much obliged to him, and hope at his ninetieth anniversary some of the younger men will do as much for him."

After this, Longfellow, almost as shy of such functions as Whittier, could do no less than read the answering "Response," which is here printed with the accompanying prefatory note, as it appears in Whittier's revised works.

"RESPONSE

"On the occasion of my seventieth birthday in 1877, I was the recipient of many tokens of esteem. The publishers of the *Atlantic Monthly* gave a dinner in my name, and the editor of *The Literary World* gathered in his paper many affectionate messages from my associates in literature and the cause of human progress. The lines which follow were written in acknowledgment.

"Beside that milestone where the level sun,
Nigh unto setting, sheds his last low rays
On word and work irrevocably done,
Life's blending threads of good and ill outspun,

I hear, O friends! your words of cheer and praise,
Half doubtful if myself or otherwise.
Like him who, in the old Arabian joke,
A beggar slept and crowned Caliph woke.
Thanks not the less. With not unglad surprise
I see my life-work through your partial eyes;
Assured, in giving to my home-taught songs
A higher value than of right belongs,
You do but read between the lines
The finer grace of unfulfilled designs."[1]

Emerson then read with his unique impressiveness Whittier's "Ichabod"; Holmes and Stoddard read poems, and speeches were made by Story, Howells, Norton, Warner, and myself. So complete was the success of the enterprise, then rather a novel one in Boston, that it was followed by a similar entertainment on the seventieth birthday of Holmes, with the curious difference that Whittier, a lifelong advocate of the equality of sexes was greeted on this occasion by men only, while the far more conservative Holmes saw before him a brilliant gathering of both men and women. I think it was the general agreement that the second celebration was even more successful than the first.

Whittier of course made no speech on this later occasion, but he sent to the *New York Critic* on a subsequent birthday of his old friend, a summary of his qualities that was better than a speech. It is as follows:—

"To the Editor of the New York 'Critic.'

"8th mo., 1884.

"Poet, essayist, novelist, humourist, scientist, ripe scholar, and wise philosopher, if Dr. Holmes does not at the present

[1] "Works," II. 168, 169.

time hold in popular estimation the first place in American literature, his rare versatility is the cause. In view of the inimitable prose-writer, we forget the poet; in our admiration of his melodious verse, we lose sight of 'Elsie Venner' and 'The Autocrat of the Breakfast-Table.' We laugh over his wit and humour, until, to use his own words, —

> "'We suspect the azure blossom that unfolds upon a shoot,
> As if Wisdom's old potato could not flourish at its root;'

and perhaps the next page melts us into tears by a pathos only equalled by that of Sterne's sick Lieutenant. He is Montaigne and Bacon under one hat. His varied qualities would suffice for the mental furnishing of half a dozen literary specialists. To those who have enjoyed the privilege of his intimate acquaintance, the man himself is more than the author. His genial nature, entire freedom from jealousy or envy, quick tenderness, large charity, hatred of sham, pretense, and unreality, and his reverent sense of the eternal and permanent, have secured for him something more and dearer than literary renown — the love of all who know him. I might say much more; I could not say less. May his life be long in the land!"

The wish was fulfilled, and Holmes was the only one of Whittier's immediate circle of literary companions who outlived him.

In private life Whittier was, during these years, in many respects most fortunate, or at least as near it as a lonely man can be. In his own house at Amesbury he had the friendly companionship of Judge Cate and wife; and during the summers he was for twelve years with his cousins, Joseph and Gertrude W. Cartland, at Intervale, N.H., or elsewhere among the White Mountains or wandered so far seaward as to be a housemate of Celia Thaxter and other cultivated persons at Appledore among the Isles of Shoals, or

Greenacre in Maine. In winter he made his home — after the marriage of his niece who had kept house for him — at Oak Knoll in Danvers, a beautiful estate where his cousins Mrs. Woodman and the three Miss Johnsons resided; a place made more interesting to him from the fact that it had been the abode of the Rev. George Burroughs, who had been put to death during the witchcraft excitement, two centuries before. He always, however, retained his home and citizenship in Amesbury, went thither to vote and to attend Quarterly Meetings, and toward the end of his life made it his residence once more.

One of his enjoyments in later years was in recalling his memories of his early friend Lydia Maria Child, whose experience of life had so much in common with his own; and in serving her memory by editing a volume of her letters (1883). In his introduction he says of her "Appeal for that class of Americans called Africans": —

"It is quite impossible for any one of the present generation to imagine the popular surprise and indignation which the book called forth, or how entirely its author cut herself off from the favour and sympathy of a large number of those who had previously delighted to do her honour. Social and literary circles, which have been proud of her presence, closed their doors against her. The sale of her books, the subscriptions to her magazine, fell off to a ruinous extent. She knew all she was hazarding, and made the great sacrifice, prepared for all the consequences that followed. . . . It is not exaggeration to say that no man or woman of that period rendered more substantial service to the cause of freedom, or made such a great renunciation in doing it."

Nor is it exaggeration to say that no man or woman of that period was so fairly to be classed with her as was the writer of these words. She had before this time passed away, having died in 1880.

A speech before the Essex Club by Senator Hoar, a few weeks before Whittier's eightieth birthday, brought forth one of the most striking tributes ever paid to an American author. It consisted of Senator Hoar's speech, followed by the signatures of all the Essex Club, of fifty-nine United States Senators, the entire bench of the Supreme Court of the United States, — headed by Chief Justice Waite, — of Speaker Carlisle of the House of Representatives, and three hundred and thirty-three Members of the House, coming from every state and territory in the Union. To these were added the names of many private citizens of distinction, such as George Bancroft, Robert C. Winthrop, James G. Blaine, and Frederick Douglass. In that same year (1887) a companion tribute came in more concentrated form across the ocean.

In 1887, Mr. George W. Childs, of Philadelphia, generously offered to defray the expense of a Milton memorial window in St. Margaret's Church, London. The offer was accepted, and in October of that year, Archdeacon Frederick W. Farrar wrote to him as follows: —

"The Milton window is making good progress. It will be, I hope, magnificently beautiful, and both in colouring and design will be worthy of your munificence, and worthy of the mighty poet to whose memory it will be dedicated. The artists are taking good pains with it. I sent you an outline of the sketch not long ago. Before the end of the year I hope to send you a painting of the complete work. Messrs. Clayton and Bell are putting forth their best strength, and promise me that it shall be finished before the end of the Jubilee Year. When it is put in, I shall make your gift more universally known. Mr. Lowell wrote me a quatrain for the Raleigh window. I can think of no one so suitable as Mr. J. G. Whittier to write four lines for the Milton window. Mr. Whittier would feel the fullest sympathy for the great Puritan poet, whose spirit was so completely that of the Pilgrim Fathers. I have always loved and admired Mr. Whittier's poems. Could you ask him as a kindness to yourself and to me, and as a tribute to Milton's memory, if he would be so good as to write this brief inscription, which I would then have carved in marble or otherwise under the window. The same tablet will also record that it is your gift to the church of the House of Commons, which was dearer to Milton than any other."

Mr. Childs forwarded this letter to Mr. Whittier, who accepted the commission, and composed the following quatrain: —

"The new world honours him whose lofty plea
For England's freedom made her own more sure,
Whose song, immortal as its theme, shall be
Their common freehold while both worlds endure."

These lines were sent to Mr. Childs, to be forwarded to Archdeacon Farrar, in a letter from Mr. Whittier of which the following is a copy: —

"I am glad to comply with thy request and that of our friend Archdeacon Farrar. I hope the lines may be satisfactory. It is difficult to put all that could be said of Milton into four lines. How very heartfelt and noble thy benefactions are! Every one is a testimony of peace and good will. . . . I think even such a scholar as Dr. Farrar will not object to my use of the word 'freehold.' Milton himself uses it in the same way in his prose writings, viz., 'I too have my chapter and *freehold* of rejoicing.'"

Mr. Whittier suggested to Dr. Farrar that if thought preferable the word "heirloom" might be substituted for "freehold." This is the Archdeacon's reply, dated Jan. 2, 1888: —

"First let me express the wish that God's best blessings may rest on you and your house during this New Year. My personal gratitude and admiration have long been due to you for the noble influence you have exercised for the furtherance of forgotten but deeply needed truths. I have myself endeavoured to do something to persuade men of the lesson you have so finely taught, — that God is a loving Father, not a terrific Moloch. Next let me thank you for the four lines on Milton. They are all that I can desire, and they will add to the interest which all Englishmen and Americans will feel in the beautiful Milton window. I think that if Milton had now been living, you are the poet whom he would have chosen to speak of him, as being the poet with whose whole tone of mind he would have been most in sympathy. . . . Unless you wish 'heirloom' to be substituted for 'freehold,' I will retain the latter as the original."

Whittier was taken with his last illness while visiting at the house of his friend, Miss Sarah A. Gove of Hampton Falls, N.H., seven miles from Amesbury. Miss Gove was the daughter of an old friend; of "that saintly woman whom we associate with one of the most spiritual and beautiful of his poems, 'A Friend's Burial.'"[1]

On September 3, he had a slight paralytic stroke which produced a difficulty in taking food or medicine, and it was plain that he could not be removed to Amesbury, where he had always hoped to die. He was conscious to the last, was grateful to every one; and several times said "Love to all the world." He died in serene and quiet constancy to that feeling of affection, and had little acute pain. He lay all night in

[1] Fields's "Whittier," p. 101.

peace, and died in the morning, one of the relatives present reciting softly his poem "At Last," as he passed away. This poem, written ten years before, is his best epitaph.

"At Last

"When on my day of life the night is falling,
And, in the winds from unsunned spaces blown,
I hear far voices out of darkness calling
My feet to paths unknown.

"Thou who hast made my home of life so pleasant,
Leave not its tenant when its walls decay;
O Love Divine, O Helper ever present,
Be Thou my strength and stay!

"Be near me when all else is from me drifting;
Earth, sky, home's pictures, days of shade and shine,
And kindly faces to my own uplifting
The love which answers mine.

"I have but Thee, my Father! let Thy spirit
Be with me then to comfort and uphold;
No gate of pearl, no branch of palm I merit,
Nor street of shining gold.

"Suffice it if — my good and ill unreckoned,
And both forgiven through Thy abounding grace —
I find myself by hands familiar beckoned
Unto my fitting place.

"Some humble door among Thy many mansions,
Some sheltering shade where sin and striving cease,
And flows forever through heaven's green expansions
The river of Thy peace.

"There, from the music round about me stealing,
I fain would learn the new and holy song,
And find at last, beneath Thy trees of healing,
The life for which I long."

1882.[1]

The following simple and touching picture of his funeral is from the historical address on Whittier by his friend Robert S. Rantoul.

"I attended his funeral. The day was ideal — a cloudless September sky above, a wealth of autumn beauty all about. No word was uttered in speech or song that day but it was apt, spontaneous, sincere. I think I never joined in obsequies more fit. Their simplicity was absolute. The poet Stedman spoke as few men can, and with a grace and aptness which, perfect as they were, yet seemed unstudied. It was hard to say whether deep feeling or critical characterisation were the leading quality of his words. And the Hutchinsons sang 'Lay Him Low' as if it had been written for themselves and for the day; and the sister Friends, whose habit of speech in public gatherings made the part they took seem only the expected thing, bore testimony from out the depths of their experience to what the world had come at last to know."

[1] "Works," II. 333.

INDEX

o

The More Recent Issues of the Series

English Men of Letters

Edited by JOHN MORLEY

MATTHEW ARNOLD	By HERBERT W. PAUL
SIR THOMAS BROWNE	By EDMUND GOSSE
ROBERT BROWNING	By G. K. CHESTERTON
FANNY BURNEY	By AUSTIN DOBSON
GEORGE CRABBE	By ALFRED AINGER
MARIA EDGEWORTH	By EMILY LAWLESS
GEORGE ELIOT	By SIR LESLIE STEPHEN
EDWARD FITZGERALD	By ARTHUR C. BENSON
WILLIAM HAZLITT	By AUGUSTINE BIRRELL
THOMAS HOBBES	By SIR LESLIE STEPHEN
ANDREW MARVELL	By AUGUSTINE BIRRELL
THOMAS MOORE	By STEPHEN GWYNN
WILLIAM MORRIS	By ALFRED NOYES
WALTER PATER	By ARTHUR C. BENSON
SAMUEL RICHARDSON	By AUSTIN DOBSON
DANTE GABRIEL ROSSETTI	By ARTHUR C. BENSON
JOHN RUSKIN	By FREDERIC HARRISON
WILLIAM SHAKESPEARE	By WALTER RALEIGH
ADAM SMITH	By FRANCIS W. HIRST
SYDNEY SMITH	By GEORGE W. E. RUSSELL
JEREMY TAYLOR	By EDMUND GOSSE
LORD TENNYSON	By SIR ALFRED LYALL
JAMES THOMSON	By G. C. MACAULAY

Each in cloth, 12mo, 75 cents net; by mail, 84 cents

IN PREPARATION

JANE AUSTEN	By H. C. BEECHING
MRS. GASKELL	By CLEMENT SHORTER
BEN JONSON	By GREGORY SMITH
CHARLES KINGSLEY	By G. K. CHESTERTON

PUBLISHED BY

THE MACMILLAN COMPANY

SIXTY-FOUR TO SIXTY-SIX FIFTH AVE., NEW YORK

The American Extension of the Well-known Series

English Men of Letters

NOW INCLUDES

WALT WHITMAN
By GEORGE R. CARPENTER, Professor of Rhetoric in Columbia University.

RALPH WALDO EMERSON
By GEORGE EDWARD WOODBERRY, Professor of Comparative Literature in Columbia University.

JOHN GREENLEAF WHITTIER
By THOMAS WENTWORTH HIGGINSON.

WILLIAM HICKLING PRESCOTT
By HARRY THURSTON PECK, Ph.D., Columbia University.

WILLIAM CULLEN BRYANT
By WILLIAM ASPENWALL BRADLEY.

Each is bound attractively in blue cloth, library gilt, 12mo
Price, 75 cents net; by mail, 84 cents

IN PREPARATION

BENJAMIN FRANKLIN
By OWEN WISTER, Author of "The Seven Ages of Washington," etc.

JAMES RUSSELL LOWELL
By HENRY VAN DYKE, D.D., LL.D., Murry Professor of English in Princeton University.

EDGAR ALLAN POE
By W. P. TRENT, Professor of English Literature, Columbia University, Editor of "Southern Writers," etc.

PUBLISHED BY
THE MACMILLAN COMPANY
SIXTY-FOUR TO SIXTY-SIX FIFTH AVE., NEW YORK